PRAGUE

Editorial Directors
Soline Massot, Anne Zweibaum

Design, Layout & Cover

Christian Rondet

Translation

Edward Freeman/Portes Paroles

Copy Editor
Elizabeth Ayre

Lithography
L'Exprimeur, Paris

© Vilo Publishing, Paris 2002
25, rue Ginoux - 75015 Paris-FRANCE

ISBN: 2-87939-251-9
Printed in Italy

PRAGUE

JANA CLAVERIE
ALENA KUBOVA

WITH THE COLLABORATION OF PAVEL VAREJKA AND BENOÎT CHALANDARD

TERRAIL

Josef Sudek

View of Prague, circa 1950.

CONTENTS

Notes
Bibliography
Acknowledgements
Photographic Credits

Josef Sudek

Above: Kampa Park, circa 1950.
Opposite page: View of Prague, circa 1950.

PRAGUE

In 1900, Prague was a rapidly expanding city. Industrialization brought with it an increase in the population, which rose to half a million inhabitants. The city began to expand, and three new bridges were built between 1905 and 1914. Public transport became organized and the first electric tram made its appearance in 1891.

Bohemia was a rich region, the most industrialized in Austria-Hungary. The Czech middle classes were very prosperous, and the building of a number of lavish investment and savings banks was a sure sign of their economic power. The Czech capital was very receptive to technical progress. In 1898, there was an Architecture and Engineering Exhibition during which the first Czech feature film was shown. In 1904, the first Motor Show was held, and in 1907, the Praga automobile factory was created. In that same year, the first purpose-built cinema in Bohemia opened its doors, and by 1910, the number had grown to fifteen.

Technical progress also began to have its effect on housing. Between 1880 and 1885, the first piped water systems brought about improvements in hygiene. Electricity began to be installed in Prague apartments in the 1890s.

During this period, the city council began to devote its attention to town planning. One of its first decisions in 1885 was to demolish the insalubrious old ghetto district inhabited by a population of modest means. This was in the northern part of the old city, and it was replaced by an elegant modern development. It may be considered that the history of twentieth-century town planning in Prague began the day the first pick-ax set the "Clean up the Ghetto" program in motion.

But Prague was not just a modernizing, future-oriented city. It was also one that still bore the marks of its prestigious past: at every street corner there were reminders that Prague had once been the capital of an independent country, the Kingdom of Bohemia. The situation in 1900 was very complex. Bohemia was part of Austria-Hungary, and Prague was merely a provincial capital. Furthermore, its population was not homogeneous. The 80 percent Czech majority of the population had dominated the city council since 1861 and aspired to free itself from Vienna's influence. Thus, it was hoped, could the city regain the proud status of a true European capital and at the same time flourish as the center of Czech identity. The German and German-speaking Jewish minorities saw things differently, and there were often ugly clashes between the two ethnic groups over political and linguistic issues. Indeed, the situation sometimes became so explosive that the Austrian authorities had to proclaim a state of siege in Prague. These tensions reached their peak at the end of 1897.

Cleaning up the ghetto
1893 to 1915

Advertising
for Praga automobiles

Eliska Ecksteinová-Huzová

Dress for the afternoon,
in *Elegantiní Praha*, June 1922.

Mucha

The Pole Star, 1902, study for a series on the stars, wash and pencil.

After the fall of the Badeni government, which had tried to establish linguistic equality in Bohemia, particularly violent demonstrations took place in Prague during which German and Jewish shops were looted; martial law was declared but not before three people were killed. The situation was further complicated by purely political tensions on top of nationalist conflict: thus in 1905, 150,000 people demonstrated in Prague, calling for universal suffrage, and obtaining it two years later.

The Czechs had a subordinate political status but demanded the same autonomous status as the Hungarians. Their campaign during the second half of the nineteenth century resulted in the asserting of what one might call "Czechness," a specific Czech identity in cultural and linguistic matters going back a long time. The movement reached a peak in the 1880s with the building of the National Theater (paid for by public subscription) and the National Museum, the latter closing off the end of Wenceslas Square. This trend continued until the end of the First World War. Between 1903 and 1912, the "Municipal House" (i.e. of the City of Prague) was built, and symbolic monuments were erected. These includes statues of Saint Wenceslas, the patron saint of Bohemia, in 1912, and Jan Hus, the pre-Reformation martyr burned at the stake in Konstanz in 1415, which was inaugurated in 1915. All of this activity marked the reclaiming of the capital by the Czechs.

The intense cultural life of the city, although rich and original, was in fact more complex than is generally realized. The University of Prague was divided into two, a German part and a Czech part, in 1882. Intellectuals from the two linguistic communities had totally separate cultural heritages, studied in separate places, and frequented different theaters and cafés. This cultural segregation is best illustrated by the case of Franz Kafka. Paradoxically, although he is without a doubt the most famous writer Prague has ever produced, in his time he was practically unknown outside the limited orbit of the German-speaking Jewish community in Prague. He lived in a sort of parallel world and published his work in Leipzig. Yet it was not totally unknown for the two communities to work together. Thus the Group of Eight, that brought twentieth-century avant-garde painting to Prague, included Czechs as well as Germans.

Viteslav Nechleba

Poster for the 31st Exhibition of the Mánes Association, "The Independents,"
1910, Museum of Decorative Arts, Prague.

Vladimir Zupansky

Poster for the Rodin Exhibition,
1902, Museum of Decorative Arts, Prague.

Artists as well as the general public in Prague were well informed about literary and artistic trends in the rest of Europe. The *Modern Review* published amongst other things reports on exhibitions in Paris and familiarized its readers with the work of turn-of-the-century artists such as Odilon Redon, Félicien Rops, Aubrey Beardsley, Edvard Munch and James Ensor. The Mánes Society, to which most of those active in the fine arts belonged, was tuned in to the rest of Europe. It brought the latest developments in French, German and Scandinavian art to the notice of the Prague public via its journal *Free Tendencies* and the holding of a series of exhibitions of the work of foreign artists, notably Rodin in 1902 and Edvard Munch in 1905. These exhibitions gave a considerable stimulus to the growth of an original and mature art movement in Prague.

Until the end of the 1880s, the major concern of Prague artists was to assert the identity of the Czech nation. After 1895, that was no longer in doubt and artists were free to express their personal individuality rather than their nationality. Many of them naturally trained in the capital, Vienna, as well as Munich and Paris (where a great number of them had studied ever since 1852). Imbued with the cosmopolitan spirit of a city situated in the heart of Europe, they followed the "modern style" that was currently flourishing in Vienna, Brussels, Paris, Munich, Barcelona, and other cities which went by the name of Secession in Central Europe and Art Nouveau in France. At first linked to Viennese Secession, Prague Art Nouveau harmonized wonderfully with the gothic-baroque setting of the city and developed a specifically Prague form. The Czech nation directly contributed, furthermore, to the richness of Parisian Art Nouveau due to the influence of one of its leading figures, Alfons Mucha (1860-1939).

Prague Art Nouveau was "total" art. Its practitioners designed not just the facades of buildings but also sculptures, murals, mosaics, stained glass windows, wrought-ironwork, posters, furniture, vases, jewelry, etc. František Drtikol (1883-1961), one of the great twentieth-century masters of Czech photography, made portraits and female nudes in an undeniably Art Nouveau spirit between 1900 and 1913.

All over Prague, architects like Osvald Polívka (1859-1931) and the "father" of modern Czech architecture himself, Jan Kotěra (1871-1923), built apartment blocks, the head offices of banks and insurance companies, publishing houses, hotels, a department store and even the main railway station, all of which were decorated with floral designs and female profiles. The greatest example of Prague Art Nouveau is the "Municipal House," built between 1903 and 1912 to the designs of Osvald Polívka and Antonín Balšánek (1865-1921). It was designed to be a lavish and refined setting for Czech high-class social and cultural life, and contains cafés, restaurants and saloons, a large concert hall-cum-ballroom, and exhibition galleries. A whole generation of artists with roots in Symbolism, such as Jan Preisler (1872-1918) and Alfons Mucha, designed the decoration, and a specific Czech character was part of the brief. Art Nouveau had one last official flourish in 1918, when Czechoslovakia became independent and Alfons Mucha was commissioned to design the new country's first postage stamps and banknotes.

Auguste Rodin

Inauguration of the Rodin Exhibition in the Mánes Pavilion, Prague, 1902.

In sculpture, the eminently poetic work of Jan Stursa (1880-1925), who was also Symbolist and eclectic in his origins, created work presenting an almost dematerialized vision of the human body. His *Melancholy Girl* is regarded as one of the most characteristic pieces of Czech Art Nouveau sculpture. The Municipal House was completed in 1912 at a time when the Art Nouveau fashion was in decline and most Prague architects had already moved on to something more sober, or "modern," or even begun to embrace Cubism. Just as in other places, it is a mistake to think that the history of art in Prague progresses in a straight line. Between 1900 and 1910, painting could be seen in that city covering a range of styles from the Impressionism of Antonín Slaviček (1870-1910), who painted a series of views of Prague in the Impressionist manner during that decade, to the isolated abstract experiments of Alois Bílek (1887-1961) via the neo-Symbolism of Jan Zrzav (1890-1977) and Josef Váchal (1884-1969) and the Expressionism of the Group of Eight.

Prague municipal House

Front elevation (former House of Representation), 1903-1912, Antonín Balšanek and Osvald Polívka.

Alfons Mucha

Prague municipal House, 1910-1911,
Decoration of the mayor's drawing room.

Entrance with stained glass windows,
Novàk department store, 1902, Prague.

František Kysela

Poster for the 23rd Exhibition of the Mánes Association,
"The French Impressionists," 1907, Museum of Decorative Arts, Prague.

Anna Boudova-Sucgardova

Vase, circa 1900,
Museum of Decorative Arts, Prague.

Vocational School of Turnov

Comb, shell, alabaster, silver,
Bohemian garnet, post-1900,
Museum of Decorative Arts, Prague.

Vaclav Svec

Vase, 1908,
Museum of Decorative Arts,
Prague.

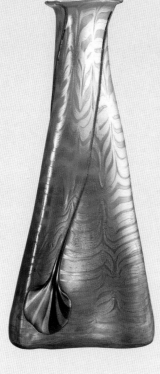

Vase, post-1900,
Museum of Decorative Arts,
Prague.

Vase, post-1900, Museum
of Decorative Arts, Prague.

In April 1907, Czech Expressionism was officially born with the first exhibition of the Group of Eight (a second followed a year later). There were five young Czech painters, including Bohumil Kubita (1884-1918) and Emil Filla (1882-1953), and three Germans. With the Eight, avant-garde art made its appearance in Prague. The group had strong links with the German group Die Brücke (The Bridge), which Kubišta actually joined in 1911. One of their main beliefs was the importance of color and they felt particular admiration for the work of Munch, Van Gogh and Gauguin. In their eyes, a painting was not a realistic representation of the external world but rather something in which intense color effects conveyed the artist's vision and his deep personal response to that external world.

Experimenting with color did not take them as far as abstraction, even though one of the great precursors of abstract art, František Kupka (1871-1957), was a Czech. Kupka in fact lived in Paris and his work was practically unknown in Prague before the First World War. The only slight impact he had was on Alois Bílek in 1913 and 1914, who had visited Kupka in Paris. Modern art in Prague included a late Symbolist current. It was geared more to introspection, spirituality, and externalized visions trawled from the depths of the subconscious than to experiments with form. It was sometimes close to anarchism and drew its inspiration variously from hermetic philosophy, oriental thought, metaphysics, spiritualism and even satanism; its artistic expression was similarly varied – drawing, engraving, pastel, painting and illustration. In 1910, several of these painters founded the Sursum Group. Among them were Zrzav and Váchal and in the words of the latter they were artists who "adored the spirituality of the Middle Ages, incunables, both the devil and God, everything that our age rejects." They were deliberately provocative, good examples being Váchal's painting *Invocation to the Devil* and Zrzav's *Antechrist*. The mystical sculptor František Bílek (1872-1941) was also associated with this movement, which was sometimes called the "second Symbolism".

Emil Filla

The Night of Love,
1907, National Gallery, Prague.

František Kupka

Piano Note – The Lake,
1909, National Gallery, Prague.

Jan Preisler

The Black Lake,
1904, National Gallery, Prague.

Frantisek Kupka

The Origin of Life, from *the Voices of Silence* cycle,
1900-1903, National Gallery, Prague.

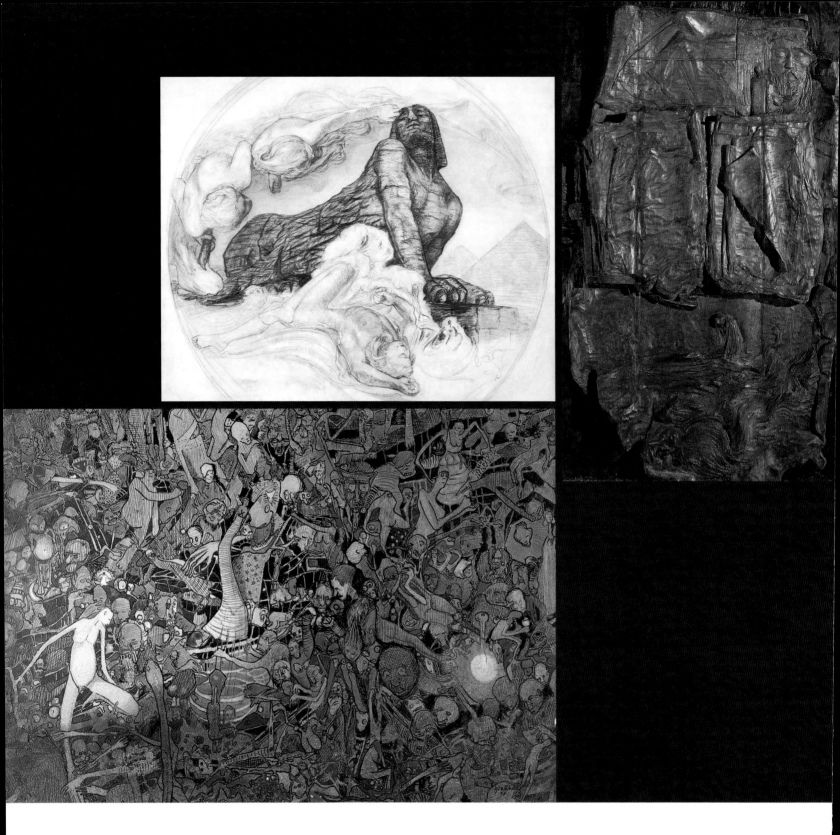

František Bilek

Untitled,
1897 (?), National Gallery, Prague.

Josef Váchal

The Plain of the Elements,
1907, National Gallery, Prague

František Bilek

The Explanation of the Word Madonna,
1897, National Gallery, Prague.

František Kupka

Fugue in Two Colors,
1912, National Gallery, Prague.

ARCHITECTURE

Peterka house, 1899-1900
Jan Kotěra designed the front elevation and Vilém Thierhier the ground plan.

opposite page
Industrial Palace

1890-1891. Bedřich Münzberger. This building, constructed almost entirely of iron and steel, was erected for the Jubilee Exhibition of 1891.

Like other European capitals, Prague significantly changed its architectural models in the second half of the nineteenth century[1]. The traditional "historical" styles were called into question, giving way to a new eclecticism, and much attention was paid to the question of ornament. Reacting to political and cultural domination by the Austro-Hungarian Empire, Prague also raised the issue of its national identity. This legitimate claim was the focus of intellectual life[2] and had a number of new prestigious public buildings[3] as one of its consequences. Despite these converging trends, it was not until the Paris World's Fair of 1900 that Bohemia was identified as a nation, with Vienna as its capital and Prague as a provincial city. Yet Czech was still not an official language, and literature and theater were not in a position to make a clear statement about Czech culture. Could architecture do any better?

The intention of doing so came via what in Prague as well as in other European capitals[4] was known as Art Nouveau or Secession. The Jubilee Exhibition was a sign of a movement of renewal, but it is Jan Kotěra to whom credit goes for designing one of the first Prague buildings in the Secession style; the facade of the Peterka House was immediately hailed by the Mánes artists. Kotera was a young man who had trained with Otto Wagner and won the Grand Prix de Rome, and was to be a leading light in Czech architecture until his death in 1923. On the site in question, although the building was on a narrow plot of land, the architect conceived the facade in three thin strips stretching upward, creating a new urban scale as regards the roofline. The decorative detail was intentionally restrained and unusual for the time in that it made no allusion to historical antecedents. The stuccowork, standing out from the smooth rendered surfaces of the facade, harmonized with the whole, giving emphasis to the spandrels of the lintels, upper entablature and gables by means of geometrical floral motifs silhouetted against the rendering. The elegant ironwork of the balconies was in characteristic Art Nouveau style.

The champions of modernity ask the question: just how far should the contemporary arts go in breaking free from historical styles? Josef Fanta's response was the main railway station. The facade and overall design were classical, but an eclectic range of styles, materials and polychrome detail was superimposed upon them. The main concourse displayed the full range of architectural and decorative refinements currently available (two- and three-dimensional surfaces molded and painted, stucco, metalwork, and a wide color range).

One of the ambitions of the Art Nouveau movement was to achieve totally coherent design aesthetically, with the artist/architect being responsible for the furniture as well as the building and making use of vernacular talents being used whenever possible. The Municipal House takes decorative detail to an extreme, calling on all the resources of Czech artists and craftsmen. The building is deliberately not aligned with its neighbors at floor level in order to permit a view of the nearby medieval tower and preserve that building's status as a city gate, underscoring the concern for the city's heritage. Osvald Polívka, one of the two architects, designed numerous Secession buildings and was a leading exponent of the style, even if his work frequently incorporated historical features. A purer and more committed approach can be seen in the Hôtel Europa, and its neighbor, the Hôtel

Prague Municipal House

(details),
1903-1912.
Antonín Balšánek and Osvald Polívka.

Prague Municipal House

(Former House
of Representation),
1903-1912.
Antonín Balšánek and
Osvald Polívka.
Powder Tower in
the background, one
of the gates of the
medieval fortifications.

Meran. The lavishness of the decoration of the facades continues in the café inside. The visitor enters an almost bewildering world of swirling decor, free-flowing flower motifs and sculptures in multi-colored plasterwork, with long, sinuous "whip-like" shapes in metal and wood[5]. The Europa explores the geometrical variation of Art Nouveau: the decor makes sophisticated use of right angles and arcs of a circle, which echo the architectural features and underline the rationality of the ground plan and elevations.

Although these architectural achievements are outstanding, they are far from rare in Prague. Art Nouveau is widespread throughout the city, most often in the heart of the historical districts and in a variety of types of building (apartment blocks, commercial enterprises of different sorts, administrative centers, etc). It can be systematically applied to whole facades and interiors, and also added to fin de siècle buildings superficially via the detail of ironwork, ceramics, mosaics, etc. It even commits certain large-scale excesses (the Svatopluk Čech Bridge, or by the sheer number of buildings, the Parizská Trida Boulevard and the Masaryk Quay, for example). Art Nouveau died out in Prague as elsewhere just before the First World War, a victim no doubt of a decorative fantasy that would always be vulnerable to the fickleness of taste.

Hôtel Europa

1903-1905.
Bedřich Bendelmayer, Bohumil Hübschmann
(or Hypšman) and Jan Letzel.
The powerful arabesques sweep across
the facade, the design of which is neatly
symmetrical (window bays, cornices, piers).

Hôtel Europa. The café

A view showing the precious materials, avant-
garde furniture and richness of
the woodwork and light fittings.

Entrance

Novàk department store,
Osvald Polívka, 1902, Prague.

J. NOVÁK

30

699
NOVÉ MĚSTO
PRAHA 1

Main Railway Station – "Wilson Station"
1901-1909.
Josef Fanta.

Novàk Building
(former department store), side view,
1901-1904.
Osvald Polívka.

Novàk Building

(former department store),
Detail of facade,
1901-1904.
Osvald Polívka.
The mosaic rural scenes extolling
a pastoral idyll are typical of the bucolic side
of Art Nouveau. They are in fact an allegory
of trade and industry.

The Svatopluk Čech Bridge

1905-1908.
Jan Koula (architect) and Jiří Soukup (engineer).

The Josef Hlávka Bridge

1909-1912.
Pavel Janák and Mencl František (engineer).
North section in concrete. Refined curves
of the roadway level, with a stone and carved
medallion design as the only decorative feature.

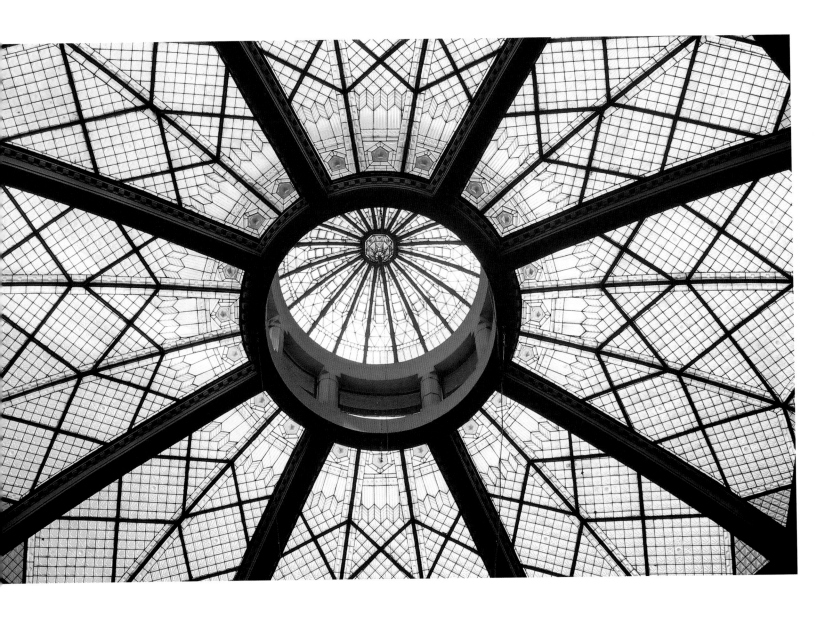

The Koruna Building

1911-1914.
Antonín Pfeiffer.
Seen from Wenceslas Square,
with the Bank of Commerce
bronzes in the background.

Double house with studio-workshop

1903-1904.
Bedřich Bendelmayer
and Emil Weichert.
View from the Prague Municipal House.

The Laichter House

1908-1909. Jan Kotěra.
Alternating smooth
and textured surfaces.

The Urbánek House

(known as the Mozarteum),
1912-1913. Jan Kotěra. Visually
the ensemble is supported
by two caryatids and topped
by a triangular pediment,
the only classical elements
in the design.

ARCHITECTURE

THE *RATIONAL BEGINNINGS*

**The Hlava Institute
of Pathology**

1913-1921, Alois Špalek.
The facade with its curved
window arrangement is
derived from a college
amphitheater design.
Originally, the top surface
of the bow-windows was
in glass to provide
the maximum lighting
for the autopsy rooms.

About the time of the Peterka House feat, Kotěra gave a fresh impetus to architecture. He was completely committed to what was going on elsewhere in Europe and absorbed the teaching of Wagner[6] and of other big names in the profession in the West. He chose above all to take popular art into account in order to be familiar with building methods and local materials. He also incorporated topographical and climatic data, as well as data concerning the purpose of the building. In short, "the purpose, the mode of construction and the location are the driving forces; the form of the building is their result."[8] Thus he had a double approach: a vernacular Czech-inclined tendency, as well as a rationalist inclination looking toward a new universal architecture. He was highly ambitious but did not get commissions measuring up to his ambitions, so had to be content with modest projects. His own villa and that of the sculptor Sucharda could be described as rational buildings in terms of layout (with the primacy of function resulting in asymmetry and volumes projecting externally), with a sober interior design and use of materials: unsculpted stone surfaces, bare brick, undecorated rendering, etc; yet each of these materials received a decorative treatment by its patterned arrangement or by its textured or polished finish. Kotěra used this style again for the Laichter House and then the Urbánek House: the elevation is bordered by a lateral projection or lip, which gives it the appearance of a framed picture, in which the canvas is the patterned or painted brickwork. With its modest use of materials and pure lines and decorative detail, this facade is thus not devoid of subtlety; if architecture is required to be true to materials, that still does not mean that it has to reveal its structural framework.

The final verdict is very positive: by displaying the building materials to the best advantage, dissociating the traditional major volumes (expressing the way space is organized) and rationalizing the plan, this current of thought[9] heralded the modernity of the avant-garde of the 1920s.

Jan Kotěra's Villa

1908-1909, Jan Kotěra.

The Štenc Publishing House

1909-1911. Otakar Novotný.
White glazed brick pilasters, and
curved glass string-course to give light
to the studio. The rear elevation was
restored by Pavel Šlechta in 1995.

From left to right: courtyard
of the printworks, front elevation,
street elevation.

Villa Trmal

1901, Jan Kotěra,
Front elevation, rear elevation.

Villa

1907-1908. Dušan S. Jurkovič.

Otto Gutfreund

Anguish
1911, National Gallery, Prague.

Photograph of the second exhibition
of the artists and sculptors group
in the Prague municipal House,
installation by Josef Gočár, Prague, 1912.

The artists and sculptors group:
Top row (left to right): Beneš, Gutfreund,
J. Capek, Chochol, K. Čapek.
Middle row: Gočár, V. Dvořák,
V. Hofmann, Janák.
Bottom row: F. Langer, J. Thon, ?

Photograph of the collector
Vincenc Kramář, in his
apartment. Behind him
are Picasso's *Self-portrait*
(1907), *Mandoline and
Absinth* (1911), *Woman
with a Guitar*.

PRAGUE
CUBISM 1910-1918

From 1909 onward, young Czech artists became particularly interested in Cézanne and devoted much attention to the question of form. At the 1910 exhibition of work by the artists of the Salon des Indépendants, organized by the Mánes Society, the City of Prague even purchased Derain's painting, *The Bath* out of the proceeds of a collection held by artists in Prague cafés. They were increasingly fascinated by the experiments of Braque and Picasso. Several artists, such as Kubita, Filla, Josef Capek (1887-1945) and his brother Karel, the writer, went to Paris, as well as the collector, historian and art critic Vincenc Kramář. The latter's role was decisive. By forming a sizeable collection of Picasso's paintings and making them available for study by Prague artists, and backing them up with theoretical writings, he became an ardent champion of Analytical Cubism. The Prague art scene was extremely receptive and became the birthplace of a very original synthesis of Cubism and Expressionism and of a Cubist style of architecture unique in the world.

In 1911, the younger generation of artists decided to form a breakaway organization from the Mánes Society, the Visual Arts Group, whose members included painters, a sculptor, architects, draftsmen, a theoretician and writers; it was to publish its own journal, *Art Monthly*. That same year, one of the members of the group, Josef Gočár (1880-1945), designed one of the first Cubist buildings in Prague, a large store called the House of the Black Madonna, which today houses the Museum of Czech Cubism. These artists were fascinated by the problem of form, and created a distinctively Prague style that is sometimes called "Cubo-Expressionist". Although not all writers on the subject accept the term, it conveys the spirit of this modern Czech art form very well, especially in painting. For whereas Cubism in Paris is sometimes nothing more than a cold formal exercise in breaking down reality, Prague Cubism is generally imbued with a spiritual or existential mood which comes out in the choice of certain themes, for example Procházka's *Prometheus* or Kubišta's *The Hanged Man*. In painting as well as in architecture, Prague Cubism has its roots in the baroque. Only Emil Filla really adopted the approach of the Analytical Cubists Picasso and Braque, even if he was seldom as austere as they were chromatically. In 1914, after he parted company with the Visual Arts Group, Josef Čapek attacked him for his servile allegiance to French models during a hostile debate between the two factions making up Czech Cubism.

Josef Gočar

Book cabinet, 1912,
Museum of Decorative Arts, Prague.

Antonín Procházka

Design for wardrobe,
1916. Moravian Gallery, Brno.

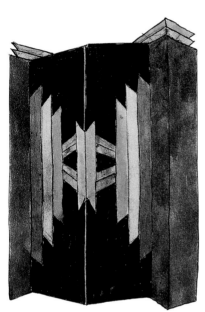

Pavel Janak

Desk, 1911-1912,
Museum of Decorative Arts, Prague

Josef Gočar

Furniture,
September 1912.

Pavel Janák

Chair
1911-1912,
Museum of Decorative Arts, Prague.

Design for dressing table,
Museum of Decorative Arts, Prague.

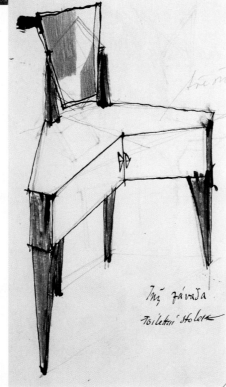

The first exhibition of the work of the Visual Arts Group took place in January and February 1912 in the Municipal House, which had only just been completed. The galleries, showcases and stands in Cubist style were designed by the architect Pavel Janák (1882-1956). A large sculpture by Otto Gutfreund (1889-1927), *Anguish*, had pride of place in the exhibition.

The Cubo-Expressionism of Prague was a "total art". It was found in all forms of expression, not just in painting, sculpture and architecture but also in interior decoration, design, furniture, ornaments, tableware, lettering, etc. Many artists were versatile exponents of the style. Thus architects such as Josef Gočar (1880-1945), Pavel Janák and Josef Chochol (1880-1956) designed buildings as well as interiors and furniture, and set up workshops in Prague where their designs could be manufactured. Their furniture had a very sculptural treatment, breaking down into separate planes and multiple surfaces while remaining coherent as furniture. Prague Cubism had a very philosophical basis to it: it was an art aiming to conquer and spiritualize matter. Form took precedence over technical and functional constraints: "The artistic consideration counts more for us than does the utilitarian aspect," was how Janák expressed it. Prague Cubists were somewhat Utopian: They believed that they were responding to the challenge of modern society, but their achievements could be appreciated only by a small number of intellectuals and rich eccentrics devoted to the avant-garde.

Nevertheless, Prague is the only European capital which can boast of Cubist-style architecture. These are buildings not put up just as prototypes out of all context, but real blocks of apartments which are still inhabited today. The buildings are spread around Prague and perfectly integrated into their surroundings. Right in the middle of Prague, in Jungmann Square, there is even a "Cubist" lamppost to be seen, which was designed by another brilliant all-rounder, Emil Králíček.

The Prague Cubist painters developed in different ways. After 1912, Kubišta became much more Futurist, introducing dynamic features into his canvases to convey action and movement, as we see in *Mountain Locomotive, Waterfall in the Alps*, and *Coastal*

Bohumil Kubišta

Waterfall in the Alps,
1912, National Gallery, Prague.

Antonín Procházka

Head of Young Woman,
1915, National Gallery, Prague.

Bohumil Kubišta

Man with a Pipe,
1910, National Gallery, Prague.

Artillery Opening Fire. A year later, he went so far as to accuse Cubism of being "superficial" because it was mainly concerned, as he saw it, with the "envelope of objects." The undeniably baroque Cubo-Expressionism of Procházka after 1915 evolved toward Orphism, experimenting with color and displaying prismatic progressions in semi-circular shapes. For others, such as Josef Čapek, Václav Špála (1885-1946) and highly Otakar Kubín (1883-1969), Cubism was above all a vehicle for a personal style, imbued with poetry, especially in the case of Capek. It was a form of grammar; they used it but did not allow it to dominate them.

As for the sculptor Gutfreund, who took the three-dimensional decomposition of forms a very long way, he can be credited with creating a number of masterpieces of European Cubist sculpture. He took this process so far that his work produced at the end of the war is almost abstract.

On the eve of the First World War, Prague was really the second great center of Cubism, and the city's avant-garde was fully integrated into the European art network. In the autumn of 1912, the second exhibition of the Visual Arts Group included work by Derain and Picasso as well as artists of Die Brücke, such as Kirchner and Schmidt-Rottluff. In the same year, several Czechs, Kubišta, Filla, Vincenc Beneš (1883-1979) and Procházka, took part in one of the most important European arts events of the time, the International Exhibition organized by the Cologne Sonderbund. The third Visual Arts Group exhibition, beginning in April 1913, actually took place in Munich in the Neue Kunst (New Art) Gallery. The fifth, in October, was held in the Berlin gallery Der Sturm (The Storm), where several of the members of the Prague Group had already participated in the prestigious first German Autumn Show that exhibited the work of seventy-five artists from twelve countries. In December 1913, the Havel Gallery in Prague hosted an exhibition of Italian Futurist work. In February 1914, just a few months before the conflagration that was going to engulf Europe, Prague was the scene of two exhibitions at the same time. One was organized by the Mánes Society and called just Modern Art, concentrating on the École de Paris: Gleizes, Metzinger, Villon, Duchamp-Villon, Archipenko, Delaunay, Mondrian, Brancusi, Dufy and Rivera. The other was by the Visual Arts Group and included work by Munch, Picasso, Derain and Braque.

Left:

Emil Filla

Salome II,
1912, National Gallery, Prague.

Above:

Emil Filla

Cubist Head,
1913, National Gallery, Prague.

Antonín Procházka

Girl Fishing, 1912, National Gallery, Prague.

Otto Gutfreund

Cubist Bust, 1913–1914, National Gallery, Prague.

Josef Čapek

Head,
1913, Private Collection, Prague.

Otakar Kubín

Human Suffering,
1914, Prague.

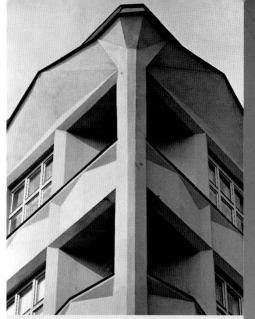

Triple House

1912-1913. Josef Chochol. Cubism playing with classical motifs, from the symmetrical design to the dominating pediment of the central section and the allegorical sculpted figures.

Opposite page and above:
Apartment block

1913-1914. Josef Chochol. The elevations create an interplay of light and shade in boldly defined sections, and create an overall harmonious effect.

ARCHITECTURE
AND CUBISM(S)

When the arabesques of the Secession style were beginning to sag, a new architectural language emerged. Josef Gočár immediately provided a striking example of it with his House of the Black Madonna. It is a building that the visitor comes across all of a sudden and is then astonished by because of its impressive, even overpowering, red mass. With the uncompromising Brutalism of the lintels and pillars, and the hugeness of the stringcourses and cornices, this building has the kind of dramatic impact that will be one of the essential features of Cubism. Another of Gocár's innovations was the use of triangular geometric shapes; this is discreet on the low surrounding wall at ground floor level and the tops of the pillars, but more visible around the door and the dormer window surrounds. There is little applied decoration: rather the ornamental effect comes from the way the structural mass is controlled and contained.

How do we account for this radical new development? It was certainly the work of young architects who refused to conform to existing modes and sought to announce their arrival in as spectacular a way as possible. In 1911, they formed the Visual Arts Group, which challenged rationalist premises.

What was at the heart of their beliefs? For one of its theoreticians, Vlastislav Hofman, "Form is absolute and comes before function, which is most of the time a variable depending upon the age"[10]. So it was a matter of inventing a form that coincided with timeless cultural values. They had their snappy formulation: "It is more accurate to say that form determines function than to say the opposite" (reversing Louis Sullivan's famous aphorism that form follows function, or the modernist teachings of Wagner). What we have here is an attempt to express architectural theory in its relationship to Czech Cubism. But how was its form to be devised? In the view of Pavel Janák[11], rethinking had to begin by challenging something as basic in architecture as the traditional roofing method, two verticals supporting a horizontal beam. Believing that a system like this was immutable caused architecture to be frozen in time, fossilized. His first argument was that there was a case for the triangular structure, and this was consistent with the Prague Cubists' enthusiasm for the pyramid, a supreme form using a minimum of material and having no superfluous mass. Secondly, Janák argued for the repetition of this motif, which is evocative of the natural process of crystallization. Finally, this overlapping geometrical form should be applied to the whole of the facade to give it unity. The principle is sufficiently abstract to be divorced from the question of the purpose of the building and the choice of building materials and their utilization.

The final concern of the Cubists was to "dramatize mass," a visual or aesthetic objective that was independent of the question of layout. Josef Chochol, in the designs of his villas and apartment blocks, resorted to a traditional arrangement of the space or the layout of the residential building along the lines of Haussmann, whereas his facades were completely Cubist. This is the case with his building in Neklanova Street, where an interplay of acute and obtuse angles is particularly striking with white rendering, creating a giant urban origami.

This aesthetic is part of the history of styles, since its laws and formal considerations are clear. In Prague, the latter are doubtless not unrelated to the city's heritage of baroque architecture, where it is also a question of blurring the boundaries of space, diffracting the human gaze and concealing the plain architectural truth of a building via the tricks of perspective. In the matter of influences, the status of Czech Cubism can be questioned vis à vis France, which inaugurated Cubism in painting. Duchamp-Villon exhibited a design for a "Cubist house" at the 1912 Autumn Salon, but it was interpreted by Hofman purely as a sculptural work as it did not seem to him to have gone beyond the traditional framework of post and lintel. In short, Czech Cubism was a distinctive phenomenon and brought much acclaim to Prague. At a time when the movement for national freedom superimposed itself upon the vision of modernity, Prague set itself up as a cultural capital while waiting to be a political capital.

Czech Cubism was essentially limited to the pre-war years and produced few buildings. It is nevertheless a fascinating subject by virtue of its uniqueness in its time and its place, and also because it

Above left and above:

The House of the Black Madonna

Josef Gočár, 1911-1912.
The building now houses the Czech Museum of Fine Arts.

anticipated certain aesthetic features of purism (notably in the sober facades designed by Chochol). After the war, Cubism was taken up again in a simplified form and incorporated in a minor way rather than applied to whole buildings. It is found in the detail of many blocks of rented accommodation built with state support. Historians have identified a renewal of Cubism in the early 1920s that can be considered to be a national style known as "Rondo-Cubism." In fact, the term was invented after the event for the purposes of classification and is not really accurate. Although there were undoubted Cubist echoes in it (the use of pure geometric shapes and lines), these quotations were superficial and inauthentic. The end result was more decorative than sculptural, applied to the facade rather than having an organic relationship with the building. The style was found in public institutions and large private companies.

The best known example is the Bank of the Czechoslovakian Legions. Josef Gočár designed it, using large and sober forms of the circle and the cylinder as his motifs. Panels or strips in the national colors of red and white enhance the entrance and the interior decoration of the foyer. In a number of respects, the design harks back to historical precedents: the conception of the facade, sculpted pillars at ground-floor level, mezzanine, monumental cornice and attic storey on top of the facade.

Another iconoclastic architect, Otakar Novotný, was more radical with his design of an urban block. The geometry of the segment, the circle and the cylinder is exploited here in a particularly pure way. The facade is devoid of all superimposed decoration (except for the capitals and the semi-circle beneath the windows). The result, somewhat paradoxically, is a combination of an uncompromisingly bare visual design bordering on Brutalism and an undeniably graphic appearance. And finally we come to the amazing Adria Palace. For his design of the facades, Janák called on Italian Renaissance palazzo motifs and also made exuberant use of circular and triangular geometric forms as well as an interplay of color. It is a strange, overornate building. The architect conceived the project on a scale that is out of keeping with the immediate surroundings but, perhaps to placate the authorities, had the good sense to design a public passageway at street level.

Adria Palace

(former Adriatic Insurance Co.), 1922-1925.
Pavel Janák and Josef Zasche.

Accommodation for teachers
1919-1921. Otakar Novotný.

The Diamond House

1912-1913. Emil Králíček, using a pyramid motif.

Street Lamp

1912-1913. Emil Králíček.

The House of the Black Madonna

Below:
The café, which has a full view of the street,
a city theater setting.
Opposite page:
Staircase.

Bank of the Czechoslovakian Legions

1921-1923, Josef Gočár.
Because of its groundplan, light airy character, rich decoration, and luxurious but rather chilly atmosphere, the foyer is often likened to Otto Wagner's post office savings bank in Vienna.

Right: Staircase.
Opposite page: Glass roof of foyer.
Below: Detail of the facade.

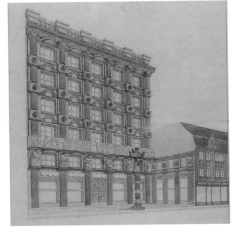

PRAGUE

DURING THE FIRST REPUBLIC

The First World War shattered Central Europe. Throughout the war, Czech émigrés, led by Masaryk, constantly pleaded the cause of the Czechs, who were drafted reluctantly into the ranks of the Austro-Hungarian army. Many deserted and allowed themselves to be taken prisoner, and whole regiments made up of deserters or prisoners were formed to fight alongside the Allies in France, Russia and Italy (the artists Kupka and Gutfreund joined the French Foreign Legion). The Czechs as well as the Slovaks were fighting for independence from Austro-Hungary, and convinced the Allies to recognize Czechoslovakia.

On October 28, 1918, a republic was proclaimed in Prague, which became the capital of a newly independent state, considered by the Czechs to be the resurrection of the ancient Kingdom of Bohemia. Czechoslovakia contained within its borders two-thirds of the industrial production of the former Austria-Hungary, mostly concentrated in Bohemia and Moravia. The country had one of the most extensive railway networks in Europe and a powerful engineering industry manufacturing locomotives, automobiles and, since 1919, aircraft. Combined with chemical and electrical engineering industries that were far from negligible, all of this meant that in the 1920s, Czechoslovakia occupied the tenth position in the world in terms of industrial production.

The main architect of Czechoslovakia's rise to economic and political success, President Masaryk steered the country firmly toward democracy. It was even an advanced one in some respects; for example, women had the vote in 1918. However, the new state was faced with a serious nationality problem, as the Czechs and Slovaks made up only two-thirds of the population, which included a sizeable German minority. Out of a total population of 13.4 million inhabitants, 3.2 million were German, mostly living around the northern fringe of Bohemia and Moravia. There was also a large Hungarian minority in the south of Slovakia. Even relations between Czechs and Slovaks were complicated. Whereas the agreement signed during the war allowed for the autonomy of Slovakia, Masaryk and the Prague

Wenceslas Square

View from the National Museum at the beginning of the twentieth century during the building works to expand Prague.

Public celebrations in Wenceslas Square at the founding of the republic on October 28, 1918.

**Josef Čapek (1887-1945)
and Karel Čapek (1890-1938)**

Tomas Garig Masaryk

(1850-1937)
First president of the Republic
of Czechoslovakia, elected
in 1918.

Above right:

Poster

(designer unknown)
advertising the Tatra
automobile, manufactured
in Bohemia.

Above far right:

J. Holy

Advertisement for
illuminated signs, 1929.

political leadership imposed upon the whole country a unitary state centered on Prague. The Czechs were soon attacked for this domineering approach. Relations between the diverse nationalities became increasingly tense, and the problem eventually led Czechoslovakia to catastrophe. The new state's main external ally was France, which organized and trained the country's armed forces, but this reliance was to prove an unfortunate illusion.

Despite a degree of prosperity, Czechoslovakia between the two world wars was not free from social problems. There were several waves of industrial unrest, culminating in a general strike in December 1920. The Communist Party of Czechoslovakia was founded in 1921, and expressed its determined opposition to the new state, which it considered to be "artificial". Things took a turn for the worse in 1933. First, it was at that time that Czechoslovakia was seriously affected by the consequences of the world economic crisis: the country's industrial production dropped to 60 percent of what it had been in 1929. Of the 849,000 inhabitants of Prague, 28,461 were unemployed.

A further complication was that the coming to power of Hitler in Germany encouraged the German minority in Czechoslovakia to express their grievances and claims. In the 1935 elections, the German Sudeten Party obtained two-thirds of the ethnic German votes, thus becoming the second-largest party in the country. The Fascist menace began to grow in central Europe's only democracy, which was more or less surrounded by hostile dictatorships of one sort or another.

On December 31, 1921, thirty-five localities had been absorbed into Prague, which henceforth covered an area of 42,395 acres. In 1930, Greater Prague had a population of nearly a million inhabitants (962,200). With the status of capital city came certain urgent requirements. Buildings had to be adapted or constructed to house a parliament, ministries, research centers. The city was more or less a permanent building site in the 1920s. The plan for a new parliament building (like certain others) was not completed, so parliament was eventually accommodated in the Rudolfinum, which had been intended for concerts and exhibitions. A residence also had to be found for the head of state, and Prague Castle was chosen. The commission to design suitably dignified accommodation and staterooms was entrusted to a Slovene architect, Jose Plecnik, between 1920 and 1934. While focusing on buildings required for state purposes, Prague did not forget its symbols. Saint Guy's Cathedral was finally completed in 1929 and re-consecrated during the solemn commemoration of the thousandth anniversary of the death of Saint Wenceslas. Between 1929 and 1932, an impressive monument was erected in honor of Zizka, the fifteenth-century Hussite leader, including an equestrian statue of that great Czech warrior designed by Bohumil Kafka (1878-1942). The tomb of the unknown warrior was also inaugurated. This commemorative ensemble was completed after the Second World War.

Josef Sudek

Kampa Park, circa 1950.

The Good Soldier Švejk
Film by Karel Lamač, 1926.

ART IN PRAGUE

DURING THE FIRST REPUBLIC

Ecstasy
Machaty

Having already been receptive to modern developments before the First World War, Prague now set about consolidating its reputation as the center of an unhesitatingly modern culture allied to technical and industrial progress. Certain functional buildings of the 1920s and 1930s, such as the Baťa Building in Wenceslas Square, designed by Ludvík Kysela (1883-1960), were showcases for artistic and industrial modernism in Czechoslovakia. New forms of expression arising from technical progress developed here as elsewhere. The first radio broadcast in the country was beamed in 1923, and there was a striking surge of enthusiasm for photography and cinema. Amateur photography societies mushroomed, and the activity flourished to such an extent that it acquired the status of an art form in its own right. The Czech Photographic Society was founded in 1924 by Josef Sudek (1896-1978) and Jaromir Funke (1896-1945). Sudek had a long career, independent of all influences; he was a sort of isolated Romantic, devoted between the wars to the realist vein of Czech photography. His favorite topic was Prague, every corner of which he photographed and in all seasons of the year. As early as 1926, Karel Lamač made the first film version of Jaroslav Hašek famous novel, *The Good Soldier Švejk*. In 1929 there were 115 cinemas in Prague, and the Barrandov film studios were completed in 1933. That same year, Gustav Machat made the first Czech film to meet with international success, *Ecstasy*, an audacious work for the times that resulted in Hedy Lamarr being recruited by Hollywood.

Situated at a crossroads in Europe, Prague was receptive to many influences, those from France, Germany (Prague artists had strong links with the Bauhaus), and Soviet Russia and even the United States because of the film industry. Prague culture was modernist, but it also had a generous utopian vision; the various avant-garde movements of the First Republic were very left-oriented, and in 1929 a large number of artists and intellectuals joined the Left Front.

After 1933, Prague was a haven for a great number of German fugitives from Nazism, and the German culture of the city was revitalized. The fugitives included some notable intellectuals, such as Bertold Brecht (whose *Threepenny Opera* was performed in 1934), Heinrich and Thomas Mann, and John Heartfield, who continued to design his famous anti-Fascist covers for the *Arbeiter Illustrierte Zeitung*, henceforth published in Prague.

Zdenek Pešánek

Kinetic light sculpture,
1936, National Gallery, Prague.

Opposite page:

Jaroslav Rössler

Smoke, 1929,
Museum of Decorative Arts, Prague.

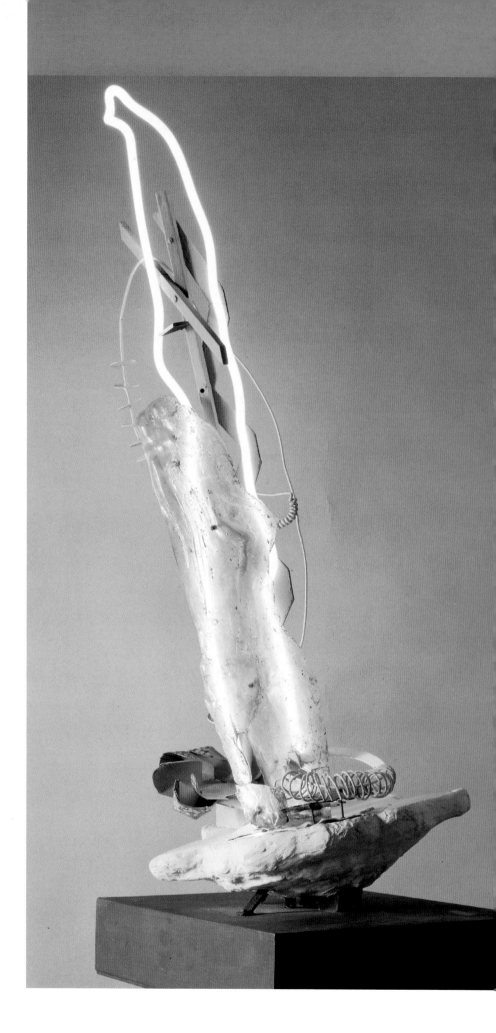

Adolf Becker

Design for vase, circa 1930,
executed by Hugo Max.

Anonymous designer

Brooch, 1925-1930.

Josef Drahonovsky

Near to the Window, 1932, Museum of Decorative Arts.

Kamenicky Senov Glassmaking School

Vase, 1930.

Jaroslav Horejc

Pallas Athena,
1920, Museum of Decorative Arts.

Bedřich Stefan

Girl with Absinthe,
1924, National Gallery, Prague.

FROM CUBISM TO ART DECO

Even before the end of the war, a group of artists associated with Cubism founded the "Obstinate" Group – notably Josef Čapek, Václav Špála, Vlastislav Hofman, and Jan Zrzavý – whose aim was to revive the dynamic artistic environment of the pre-war years. Their first exhibition took place in March 1918. But the Prague art scene had changed, not least because the leading lights of Cubism had moved out: Filla to Holland, Gutfreund to France, and Kubita was fighting on the coast of Dalmatia and was to die at the end of the year. The "Obstinates" moved away from Cubism and felt a greater affinity with the German painters of the New Objectivity movement. They held exhibitions in Berlin, Dresden and Hanover, and invited Otto Dix and Paul Klee to exhibit with them in Prague in 1921.

Yet the spirit of Cubism was not entirely dead. The year 1921 saw the publication of Kramář's important study on Cubism, and one year later there was a Picasso exhibition in Prague. The Cubist spirit lived on in certain painters such as Filla and Procházka, and in time it even had some impact on photography. In 1923 and 1924 even the classic artist Drtikol, who had always been associated with Art Nouveau, made some Cubist-inspired photographs and shots of nudes against a Cubist decor. In 1922, Jaroslav Rössler (1902-1990) created an astonishing Cubo-Futurist portrait of the dancer Ore Tarraco.

Czechoslovakia's independence naturally had consequences for Czech art. This is evident in the first instance in architecture, where the champions of Cubism such as Janák and Procházka developed what was soon considered to be the "national style" because it drew on popular art and favored the colors of the national flag, red, white and blue. It had its counterpart in painting in the work of Špála, who had been fond of folklore themes and bright reds and blues even before the war. Unlike Cubism, the "national style" – for which some modern writers have preferred the bold term "Rondo-Cubism" – regarded the circle and semi-circle as thematic. The best example of this style is the former Bank of the Legions (1921-1923), a building imbued with symbolic importance because it refers to the legions of Czechoslovakian soldiers who fought alongside the Allies from 1917 onward.

The carved friezes on the Bank of the Legions, honoring the feats of the soldiers, were the work of Otto Gutfreund. Like others, he turned his back on Cubism on moving back to Prague after the war and contributed to the more realist vein that was appearing in Czech sculpture, embracing humble, everyday social themes and myths of the modern era. Gutfreund created a whole series of figurines in polychrome terra cotta or carved wood that occupy a place half way between decorative and popular art. His work is thus part of a contemporary current of Czech art, of which typical examples are Karel Dvořák 's statuettes illustrating crafts and trades, Karel Kotrba's *Seamstress*, Otakar Švec 's famous *Motorcycle* which reflects the modernist aspirations of the Devětsil Group, and Jan Lauda's bronze *The Cleaning Lady*. Painters are part of this movement as well as sculptors, some of them being from the "Obstinate" Group, such as Josef Čapek, who painted ragpickers in 1923 and Zrzavý who in the same year did Beggarwoman, a curious work compared with what he normally did; *The Family* (1924) by František Muzika (1900-1974) bears an interesting resemblance to American realist painting of the same period. In 1924, a number of painters even founded a "Social Group".

In another direction, the "national style" in architecture and the polychrome statuettes such as the *Portrait of the Artist's Wife* by Gutfreund and the *Girl with Absinthe* by Bedřich Stefan can be seen as part of Czech Art Deco. This movement was remarkably diverse and fruitful, finding expression in sculpture, furniture, jewelry, wall hangings and drapes, ceramics, glass and crystal ornaments, porcelain, architects' models, posters, clothes and shoes. In 1925, the Czech participants at the Paris International Exhibition of Industrial and Modern Decorative Arts came back with a large number of awards. The great figure in the history of Czech Art Deco was the sculptor Jaroslav Horejc (1886-1983), who created sculpture, vases, stained glass and jewelry.

THE DRIVING FORCE IN PRAGUE'S AVANT-GARDE: DEVETSIL (NINE FORCES)

The new themes in the sculpture of Gutfreund and others at this time reflect several different artistic currents. The main avant-garde movement in Prague between the wars was Devĕtsil, which was founded in 1920. It included poets like Vítězslav Nezval (1900-1958) and Jaroslav Seifert (1901-1986), painters such as František Muzika, Josef Šíma (1881-1971, who had been living in France since 1921), Jindřich Štyrský (1899-1942), Toyen (Marie Čermínová, 1902-1980), the architects Josef Chochol, Jaromir Krejcar (1895-1949), Vít Obrtel (1901-1988), a photographer, Jaroslav Rössler, critics, including Karel Teige, theater people, writers, musicians, actors, journalists, a dancer, linguists and others. Many members were gifted in a number of ways. The great theoretician of Devĕtsil, Teige, was more than just that, being a painter, collage artist and book-cover designer.

Devĕtsil was very left-oriented and the driving force behind Prague's avant-garde movement in the 1920s. It was very diverse in its activities, even seemingly contradictory: proletarian poetry, Magic Realism and Primitivism (all of which featured in Devĕtsil's first Spring Exhibition in May 1922), Poeticism, Purism and Constructivism before some of its members eventually evolved toward Surrealism. Teige attempted to reconcile Poeticism, a "hedonist philosophy" that saw the world as a poem, based on the glorification of simple things, humor and modernism, partly inspired by Apollinaire, with Functionalism, interpreted as a virtually scientific vision of architecture inspired by the Russian experience among other things. He also tried to reconcile absolute freedom of creation with Communism.

Teige and Devĕtsil poets were fascinated by the Russian Revolution and the flowering of the avant-garde that followed. At first, they championed proletarian poetry in the Proletkult vein. But this austere phase was soon replaced by Poeticism, which drew its inspiration from cinema, the circus, sports and popular art. Unsurprisingly the movement's favorite painter was Zrzav, whose work was eminently poetic; Teige published a monograph on him in 1923. Devĕtsil published two characteristic selections of its enthusiasms, *the Devĕtsil Revolutionary Anthology and Life, Anthology of New Beauty*, and at the end of 1923 it held an exhibition entitled "Bazar of Modern Art," which was partly inspired by Dadaism.

The poetic texts of Nezval and Seifert and theoretical writings of Teige and Krejcar explained what was meant by "new beauty". It was incarnated as much by the symbols of Modernism such as automobiles, passenger liners, aircraft, skyscrapers and neon advertising, etc, as by simple things such as the circus, painted signboards and fairgrounds. In architecture, beauty resided in the purism of Le Corbusier, then in Soviet Constructivism and in Functionalism. The Constructivist ideal also came out in book covers, theater set design and photography. Entirely new forms of expression, such as image-poems, photomontage and collage evolved alongside the classic medium of painting. Some Devĕtsil members also took a lot of interest in typography and the incorporation of type within the image.

Devĕtsil was fascinated by cinema, radio, photography and all the artistic media or genres that derived from them. One of its members, the sculptor Zdeněk Pešánek (1896-1965) created kinetic sculpture using the most modern techniques and materials: electricity, neon gas, Bakelite, resin, plexiglas. He translated matter into light and movement, into "poetry for the five senses". He created two "spectrophones" or piano-generated light machines between 1924 and 1928, then an astonishing kinetic sculpture using light and sound on the roof of the Edison transformer close to the main railway station in 1929 (the first kinetic sculpture in the world).

He also designed a kinetic luminous fountain for the Czech Pavilion in the 1937 Paris World's Fair. Devĕtsil turned its back once and for all on Cubism in 1927, when Teige described it as "picturesque and decorative." Its members were totally receptive to European culture and personally in touch with kindred spirits in the avant-garde in Italy, Germany, France, Holland, Russia, Hungary, etc. They were close to the Bauhaus and De Stijl, and made Prague one of the great centers of European

Karel Teige

Opposite page from top to bottom:
- cover of the Devětsil movement magazine RED, 1927.
- Guillaume Apollinaire; *The Breasts of Tiresias,* cover and page design.
- Cover of *Radio Book.*
- Alphabet Book, 1926, cover and page design of the book.
- Portrait of Karel Teige, artist, theoretician and leader of the avant-garde movement from 1921 to 1951.

Otto Gutfreund

Head of Young Woman,
1919, National Gallery, Prague.

Vincenc Makovsky

Young Woman with Child,
1933, National Gallery, Prague.

Otakar Svec

Motorcyclist,
1924, National Gallery, Prague.

culture again. Links between Prague and Paris were strengthened, especially because of the political rapprochement between the two countries. Many Czech artists visited Paris, sometimes supported by state bursaries. Major exhibitions of French art were held in Prague (1923, 1931 and 1937) and of Czech art in Paris. But this relationship was far from exclusive. In 1921, the Rudolfinum was the setting for an exhibition of modern Italian art, notably the work of the Futurists, and Marinetti came in person to direct some Futurist performances. In 1923, Devětsil devoted an exhibition to Archipenko, and a year later the Prague Architects' Circle held a series of lectures given by leading European architects such as Le Corbusier, Loos and Gropius.

Beyond the activities of Pešánek, the theater was where the best synthesis of Poeticism and Constructivism could be found. The "Liberated Theater", which was originally the "theater section" of Devětsil, was founded in 1926 by the stage directors Jindřich Honzl (1894-1953) and Jiří Frejka (1904-1952), and is the best example of this. In the view of its creators, theater was to be a place for fantasy, gaiety and poetry. The Liberated Theater's first shows were derived from circus, cabaret and music hall routines, and were characterized by much absurd humor, parody and improvisation; the decors were often in the Constructivist style and designed by Devětsil artists like Teige, _ Štyrský, Toyen ou Šima. Plays performed included *Ubu Roi* by Alfred Jarry, *The Breasts of Tiresias* by Apollinaire and *Orpheus* by Cocteau, as well as Futurist plays by Marinetti. From 1929 onward two comic performers, Jiří Voskovec (1905-1981) and Jan Werich (1905-1980), were the leading lights at the Liberated Theater. Often what they were offering was a type of musical comedy, for which the music was composed by the jazz musician Jaroslav Ježek (1906-1942). At first it was very much a matter of improvised performances with much recourse to satirical puns and allusions to contemporary politics and cultural life. From 1935 onward, as the international political scene clouded over, the light-hearted spirit of the Liberated Theater gave way to increasingly committed plays denouncing the dangers of Fascism.

Although Devětsil had only one professional photographer among its members, Jaroslav Rössler, another member, Jindřich Štyrský, was the personification of the Poeticist mood in Czech photography. He was a great believer in the unexpected and chance encounters; he photographed shop window displays, dilapidated walls, graffiti, signs and notices, fairgrounds. He also created a set of erotic photomontages published under the title *Emily Comes to Me in a Dream*.

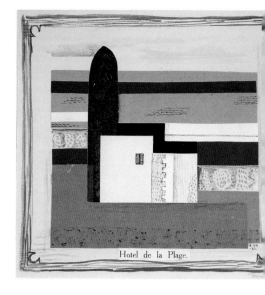

Jindřich Štyrský

The Beach Hotel,
1923, watercolor, private collection.

Poster for the Liberated Theater

Its stars Jiří Voskovec,
Jan Werich and the composer Jaroslav Ježek.

Voskovec and Werieh in performance.

Toyen

The Fair, 1925,
Oil on canvas, private collection.

Jindřich Štyrský

Chequered Landscape, 1925,
Oil on canvas, private collection

However, the Constructivist leanings of Devětsil and the principles of Poeticism influenced a number of other Czech photographers beginning with Drtikol, who had trained Rössler. In the 1920s, he made a number of nude photographs set against geometric decors in the Constructivist mode; he introduced the dynamics of movement and gave increasing importance to the interplay of light and shade. Like Drtikol, Jaromír Funke never adhered totally to any movement. He began by experiments in the Poeticist vein, with "photograms" containing ordinary objects and resembling image-poems and collages. Thus to create the effect of a face he would use a net for hair, glasses for eyes and a piece of cloth for the nose, and project the shadows of these objects onto the photosensitive paper lit by lamplight; he used the same technique for abstract compositions. Eventually he evolved to become a master of Functionalist photography. Another rigorously realist photographer was Eugen Wiškovský (1888-1964), whose specialty was industrial forms and items of Functionalist architecture. The pupil of Funke, Jaroslava Hatláková (1924-1989) revealed her Bauhaus predilection in the tight structuring and systematically geometrical control of space in her images, in particular in the series *A Solid in Space*.

František Drtikol

The Step, 1929,
Museum of Decorative Arts, Prague.

František Drtikol

Composition, 1927,
Museum of Decorative Arts, Prague.

František Drtikol

Composition, 1925,
Museum of Decorative Arts, Prague.

Toyen

Collage for the cover of André Breton's *Communicating Vessels*, translated into Czech in 1934.

THE FLOWERING OF PRAGUE SURREALISM

During the 1920s, the exponents of Poeticism were skeptical about Surrealism, although in 1925 Štyrský and Toyen presented something similar to it, Artificialism. In approximately 1930, an informal Surrealist group came into existence in Prague, led by the sculptor Ladislav Zívr (1909-1980), the painters František Gross (1909-1985) and the photographer Miroslav Hák (1911-1978). Some of these artists took part in 1937 in the exhibition of avant-garde art organized by the Theater D37, where they were in the company of Václav Zykmund (the future founder of the Ra Group, born in 1914) and members of the official Surrealist group.

In 1932, one year after Devětsil went out of existence, the Mánes Society held a big international exhibition, Poetry 32, which marked the entry of Surrealism into Prague. In addition to Czech painters close to Surrealism, like Muzika, Janoušek (1890-1943),Šíma, Štyrský and Toyen, there were a great number of artists from Paris who were Surrealists or associated with them, Arp, Dali, De Chirico, Ernst, Klee, Masson, Miro, Tanguy, all of whom were given a warm welcome by the Prague painters. Curiously, it was the poet Nezval, the most Stalinist member of Devětsil, who originally founded the Prague Surrealist group. In 1930, he brought out the journal *The Signs of the Zodiac*, which publicized the activities of Breton and the other French Surrealists, with whom he was personally acquainted. In 1934, he founded the Prague Surrealist group, among whom the most obvious members were Štyrský and Toyen, whose work drew its inspiration from dreams. Teige was at first critical of Surrealism and hesitated briefly before finally joining. The Prague group was immensely active, expressing itself in painting, collage, photomontage and photography; it had close relations with Paris, but developed autonomously. It held its first exhibition in 1935 and Breton and Éluard came to Prague the same year, which is also when the first international bulletin of Surrealism was published. Between 1935 and 1938, the year when the Czech group held its second exhibition, Prague was the second great international center of Surrealism.

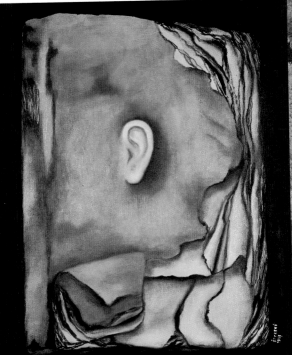

Jindřich Štyrský

The Gift, book-object
1937, oil on canvas, private collection.

Toyen

Abandoned Lair,
1937, oil on canvas, private collection.

In photography one of the first to be inspired by Surrealism was Štyrský, who produced cycles of work about the concrete irrationality of daily life, *The Man with Blinkers*, *The Frogman*, *Parisian Afternoons*, but he was far from the only one. Photographers who did not actually belong to the group nevertheless produced work that was clearly Surrealist in spirit, such as Funke with his hallucinatory window images in the *Reflections* cycle and the random encounters of *Enduring Time*. Hák's photomontage *Coleoptera-Mask* is perhaps a unique example of Dali's "paranoia-critical" method being applied to photography; and Vobecký made photomontages of some of his own photos cut up and reassembled together with engravings and other sorts of visual material. However, Surrealism in Prague was far from just confined to the official group, which a large number of artists who were close to Surrealism in spirit never joined before 1934, such as painters and sculptors like František Musika, František Janoušek, Ladislav Zívr and Zdeněk Rykr (1900-1940). Muzika, a former Devětsil member who stayed out of the official Surrealist group, had a certain "classical" style, of which Nezval wrote highly. Janoušek had leanings toward the baroque throughout the 1930s; there was a slow process of decline that culminated in apocalyptic visions such as the *Landscape with Serpents* of 1938. Zívr created "surrealist objects" out of the random juxtaposition of items and materials salvaged from garbage dumps. The work of Rykr, who exhibited with the "Obstinate" group as early as 1921, can be placed half way between imaginative art close to Surrealism and abstraction. He specialized in assemblages of tissue paper, cellophane, wood, string and sometimes even colored pebbles.

Teige regarded Surrealism as a revolutionary process aimed at subverting the established social order. Yet, there was inevitably a contradiction between the Stalinist conception of art as being absolutely subordinate to ideology and the principle of totally unfettered creative freedom that was fundamental to Surrealism. This provoked a crisis within the Prague group. When Nezval opted for subservience to the party line and tried to disband the group in 1938, Teige defended creative freedom in a publication entitled *Surrealism against the Tide*. The Prague Surrealists, who carried on as before, eventually expelled Nezval.

During the late 1930s, artists became radicalized as the international political situation deteriorated – Hitler's rise to power, the growth of Fascism, the Spanish Civil War and the increasingly imperiled status of democracy in Czechoslovakia. Some artists and intellectuals in Czechoslovakia had already been in the Left Front as early as 1929, and the range of political activities now intensified, from Liberated Theater plays satirizing Hitler to the anthology *For Spain in 1937*, published by the Support Committee for Democratic Spain to bolster the Republican government forces and including contributions by poets, musicians, artists, theoreticians and politicians. The imminent catastrophe seems to be sensed in the anguish-laden work of certain artists, such as Janoušek 's already mentioned *Landscape with Serpents*, Toyen's collection of drawings *Specters of the Desert* and Emil Filla's cycle *Animal Fights*.

Jindřich Štyrský

The Statue of Liberty,
1939, collage, private collection.

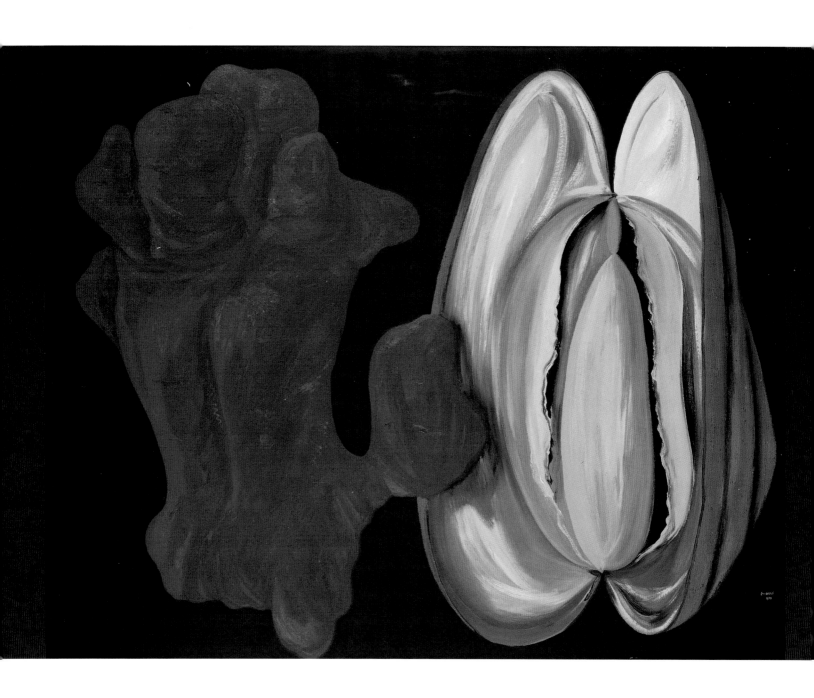

Jindřich Štyrský

Man and Woman,
1934, oil on canvas, private collection.

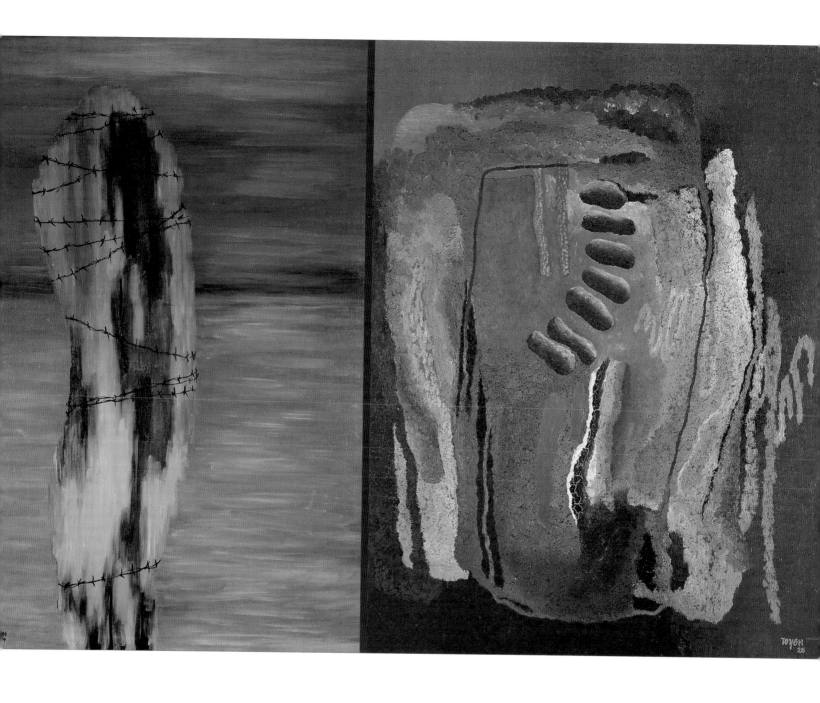

Toyen

Prometheus Bound,
1934, oil on canvas, private collection.

Toyen

Fiord
1926, oil on canvas, National Gallery, Prague.

Ladislav Zívr

Heart Incognito,
1936, National Gallery, Prague.

Opposite page:

Zdeněk Rykr

Orient,
Assemblage, 1935, National Gallery, Prague.

Josef Šima

Strange Afternoon,
1932, private collection, Prague.

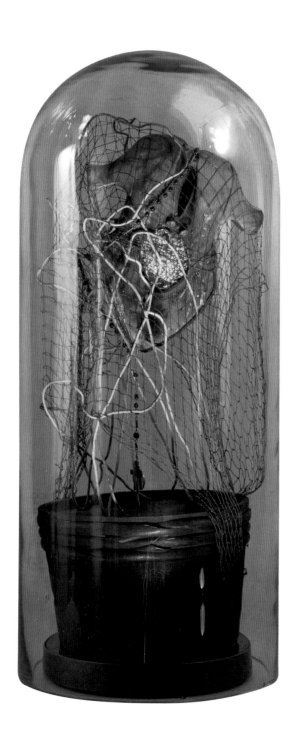

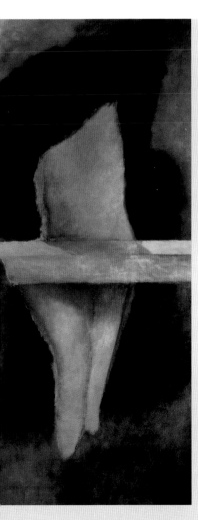

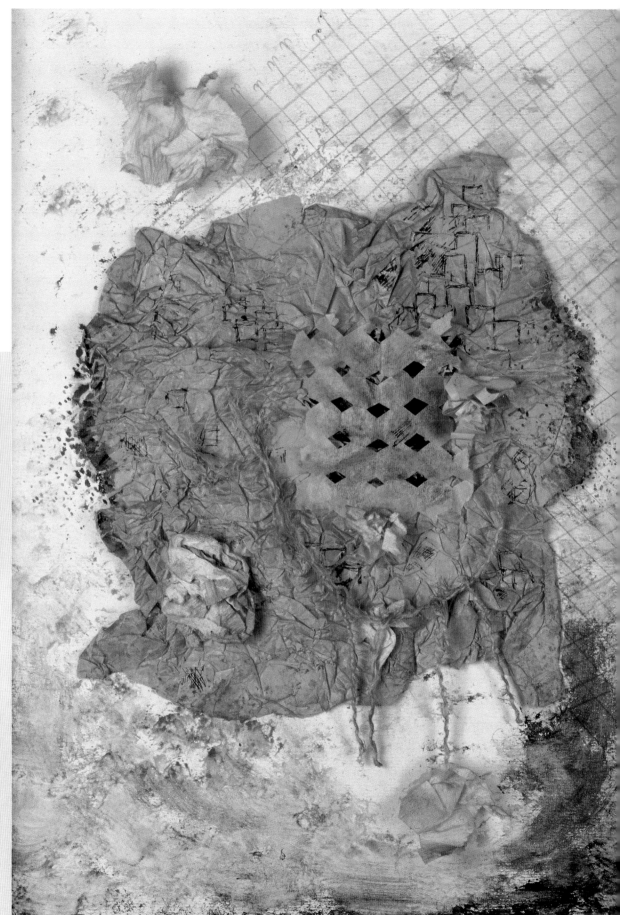

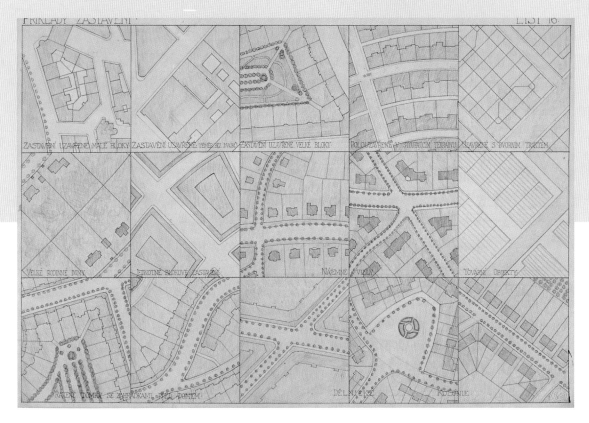

The Ideal Greater Prague

Plate 16, plot division,
Morphological study.

TOWN PLANNING BETWEEN THE WARS:
THE NEW APPEARANCE OF PRAGUE

Europe emerged from the First World War with the principle of nationhood triumphant. Prague was the capital of a nation and had to justify its metropolitan status. What condition was the city in at that time? At the end of the previous century, there had been the complete reconstruction of the Josefov Jewish district, the careful renovation of the Nové Město (new town) and the construction of stone embankments and buildings alongside the river, as well as some new bridges. Prague had been spared by the war and retained the main features of its medieval character as regards its streets and layout, into which later developments had been inserted. The specific topography of the city, with its hilly terrain and winding curves of the Vltava River, was an important factor. In 1919, a rising force in town planning, Max Urban, put forward a proposal called "An Ideal Greater Prague." Although there was no follow-up, it gives a good indication of what the new generation felt strongly about and what was at stake for Prague. Urban recommended the preservation of the historic center of the city, with work to be carried out only where it was necessary to preserve and enhance the architectural heritage. Beyond the center, he proposed an unprecedented campaign of radical redevelopment and expansion. His "ideal" metropolis would contain entire new suburbs with highly individualized architectural characters and densities of population, and capable of more or less infinite expansion. In Urban's vision, Prague would need new prestige buildings and monuments and become the headquarters for international institutions rather in the manner of the World City envisaged by Andersen and Hébrard in 1913. In this spirit he conceived the idea of a "Cosmopolis" district, complete with a lake, situated on the slopes of the Petřin and dedicated to the ideal of peace. The plans failed to impress Karel Čapek, the friend of President Masaryk and journalist of the national daily *Národní Listy*. For Čapek, rather than "monumentalize" Prague, what mattered was to attend to certain urgent needs in the city: planning laws were a necessity, for example. These would control development in the existing city as

The Ideal Greater Prague

1919. Max Urban. Plate 7.
"Comparison between the present and what is planned," plan on 1/25,000° scale. The seventy-five plates of the project covered all the scales of the design.

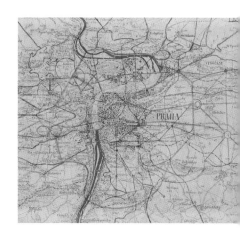

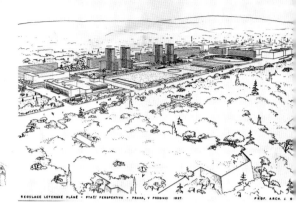

Wenceslas Square

The National Gallery in the background.

Plan for developing the Letna Plain

Architect: Josef Gočár, 1937.

The Ideal Greater Prague

The urban plan. Plate 18.
Every district is integrated into
a carefully structured network:
enormous circular junctions are
at the heart of a system of concentric
major roads and impressive
boulevards, which are carefully sited
to enhance the setting of public
buildings and monuments.

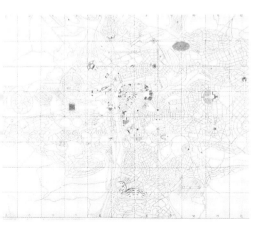

regards administration and new building, while allowing plenty of scope for individual initiatives. This was how Čapek hoped to avoid the "tyranny of plans" that contemporary urban architects were so fond of. He argued that these new planning laws were "democratic" in the new political climate of the country. The model to be followed was the American one: creating a dynamic and varied city. This of course meant the free-style development of a city like New York, not Washington, constrained by the rigid geometry of the aesthetic master plan.

A Planning Laws Commission was set up in 1920, and Max Urban was a member of it. Until that time Prague had grown by absorption: in 1890, it consisted essentially of just the Old City and New City and then in that year it absorbed the surrounding communes.[12] It was a simple administrative annexation, as the idea of a "Greater" Prague did not then exist. At the beginning of the 1920s, a prime objective was to provide extra housing (because of the influx of population) and administrative buildings and the associated infrastructure. Thus it became necessary to devise planning systems in general and to work out a master plan for Prague and its outer suburbs. The precedents were those of Greater Berlin in 1910, Haussmann in Paris and above all Otto Wagner in Vienna. Very soon, as a result of design competitions, the new Prague began to take shape. In 1922, thirty-seven communes in the two outer rings of the urban area were absorbed within the administrative authority of Prague, which set about providing them with the necessary development and infrastructure.[13] Many of these areas were rural, but there were industrial suburbs too, close to the city center, such as Libeň, Karlín and Holešovice. Major factors influencing planning and development were the complexity of the topography and the distinction between workplace and residential area. In the new agglomerations, each suburb needed thought as regards its specific composition, scale and atmosphere; if they did not already exist, they had to be devised. The density of population, ratios of built-up areas to open spaces, height of buildings relative to street widths (to improve ventilation and lighting) – all of this had to be planned and controlled. Likewise the public transport infrastructures of road, rail and tram linking suburbs and city center had to be designed. Key elements in this strategy were the railway stations, which were upgraded, and an inner city boulevard encircling the historic center. The latter prevented the need for gashes in the historic fabric caused by clearances, and made it possible to travel around quickly. The overall effect of this program was to create what Hübschmann called a "new visual profile"[14] for Greater Prague. And the ancient heart of the city was not affected, being protected: it was unthinkable that anything should be allowed to impact on the panoramic silhouette of the city, which had a historic and symbolic value (especially Hradčany hill and the castle in pride of place). The architectural heritage was considered more and more to be a cultural legacy from the past that had to be conserved.[15] The layout of the historic center was virtually untouched from this point onward and the only property development opportunities of any substance – Malá Strana and the Letná heights – went no further than the discussion stage. In twenty years, Prague was transformed into a European metropolis with a population of almost a million inhabitants on the eve of the Second World War.

ARCHITECTURE BETWEEN THE WARS:
AVANT-GARDE PROJECTS

"To live a happy and pleasant life
requires the supreme art of wasting time.
That art is poetry."
Teige [16]

Once again, it was a matter of knowing how to invent an original architecture. And once again the eternal question of the place of ornament was the preamble. This time, the fundamental questioning was radical and articulated with a political consciousness for which the Devětsil group provided the theoretical discourse. This avant-garde movement, which was founded in 1920, had a coherent ideological platform that it controlled in the manner of political parties (expulsions, godfathers, patronage) and propagated in journals.[17] The avant-garde was convinced that art had a social role to play, contributing to the organization of the world, and that architecture was the prime expression of this belief. The leader of the movement was the young Karel Teige, who published a manifesto for the new generation,[18] *Images and Prefigurations*,

Barrandov swimming pool

The diving-board, 1929-1930. Václav Kolátor. This spiral in reinforced concrete, an aerial sign of Prague's first outdoor swimming pool, was also a tribute to a vigorous avant-garde. Today it is almost destroyed by vegetation.

Photomontage

Karel Teige, 1941.

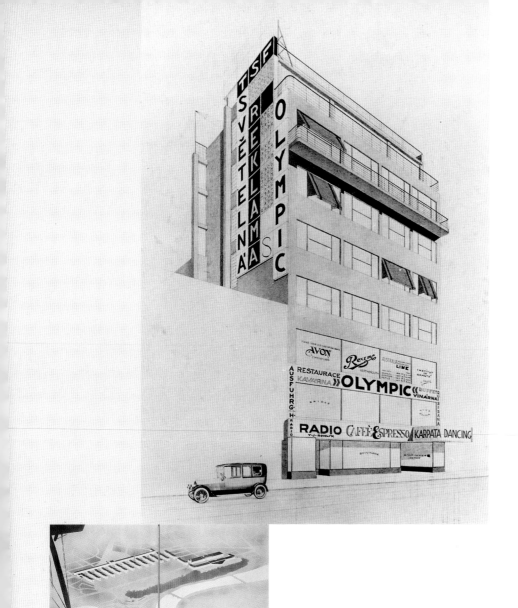

containing all his hopes for the reconstruction of the country. For Teige, "the new form of beauty is born of constructive work, which is itself the foundation of modern life". Art was henceforth to be regarded as a form of constructive work whose modernity was to be determined by its social function. In 1924, Teige published a manifesto of Constructivism which laid the foundations of this new current and of its relationship with art.[19] Translated into architectural terms, this denunciation of "art for art's sake" placed all the emphasis on the scientific aspects of building: an end to decoration and crafted fabrication, to be replaced by standard parts and production-line units. In 1922, with reference to Le Corbusier's Purism, Teige wrote that architecture was above all the art of building and not the art of decorating.[20] In the same publication, another Devětsil member, Jaromír Krejcar, presented pictures of New York skyscrapers and praised their fundamentally new design.[21] Even the old champions of Cubism shared this opinion: Josef Chochol expressed the wish that "form be stripped of the superfluous and that the language of forms should be precise and immediately comprehensible." And Josef Čapek, likewise, challenged the "national style" and argued in favor of the beauty of ordinary objects and the primacy of usefulness.[22]

This radical campaign assimilated social progress to technical progress. Lest we find this too daunting, we should remember that, although standard production-line parts may sometimes be monotonous or inhuman, the avant-garde did have a heart and was not insensitive to beauty or emotion. Devětsil developed "Poeticism"[23] in which poetry was argued to be a new art of living. According to Teige, this was a "modernized Epicureanism, in which the purpose of art is to assert, sharpen and saturate one's sensibility, leading to the greatest possible perception of the world."[24] Poeticism and Constructivism were intimately bound together, and together they posited architecture as the linchpin of the new world, uniting emotion and the wonder of creation.

We may observe finally, in keeping with the Czech avant-garde, that the Prague of the 1920s was the focus for all the main intellectual and political tendencies of European history. In 1924, in Prague and Brno, a series of lectures was organized by the journal *Stavba* on the subject of contemporary architecture. In the view of the participants, Gropius, Oud, Le Corbusier. Ozenfant, Loos and others (although Perret and Wright were absent), the future direction was clear: toward "an international art" that was not a colorless cosmopolitanism. International architecture, which was often a collective activity, could be cross-fertilizing: the Czech avant-garde, Bauhaus, De Stijl, Russian Constructivists, Le Corbusier Purists, American production-line houses and giant cities, the theories of Adolf Loos, the precursor of an architecture totally devoid of all decoration,[25] these are just a few examples, but they point to a time of intense activity. We are about to see that in the inter-war period, Prague was the scene of much architectural accomplishment in the design and building of administrative buildings, apartment blocks and private houses. The density of work achieved was exceptional (the same is true of Brno and Hradec Králové).

Project

1928. Jaromír Krejcar.
Plan for regulating the Letná plain.
View from the air.

Olympic Building

1923-1924. Jaromír Krejcar.
The building comprised a restaurant, a café and shops, as well as offices and apartments on the floors above. The ground floor has a public passageway running through it and leads to a theater. This mixed purpose concept is quite common in Prague. The Olympic cinema was restored by Jan Fišer in 1996.

Koruna Building

Frontage on Wenceslas Square.

WENCESLAS SQUARE
AND THE CITY CENTER

"WE HAVE FOUND FOR OUR POEMS BEAUTIES
QUITE NEW [...]
BE SILENT, VIOLINS, LET CAR HORNS SOUND.
MAY MAN SUDDENLY DREAM IN THE MIDDLE
OF THE CROSSROADS."
SEIFERT [26]

In the 1920s, there were several architectural styles in existence at the same time: the classical style of public buildings, variations on Cubism, rationalism and ordinary architecture. These types of architecture nevertheless often come off second best by comparison with the avant-garde forms, Constructivist, Functionalist or Purist (terms which are often interchangeable). As we have seen, this type of work was characterized by a degree of theoretical maturity, both in Prague and elsewhere in Europe, and reflected an increasing fascination with technique and its manifestations. Movement, speed, automobiles, the whole American adventure was dazzling. Movement, rhythm, electric energy, the New York scene, Broadway at night, all these things fascinated people. In Prague, jazz was all the rage, cinemas were everywhere, and the night sky was shimmering with electric advertisements and even Pesanek's illuminated kinetic sculptures.

The avant-garde dreamed of doing things on a grand scale, but had to content itself with one restricted site, at least as far as the city center was concerned. This was Wenceslas Square, with

Lindt Building
Passageway.

Lindt Building
1925-1927. Ludvík Kysela.
One of the first department stores in Prague, at the end of Wenceslas Square.

Prazdroj
PLZEŇ
LINDT
michovský
PUNČOCHY
LYONSKÝ
TOVÁRNA NA KLOBOUKY
Tisíce dárků pro tisíce přání
KVĚTINY A PÉRA
PESSL PESSL
CUKRÁRNA
ZBOŽÍ Z VLASTNÍ TOVÁRNY
NEJVĚTŠÍ ODBORNÝ ZÁVOD
LINE
MICHOVSKÝ

a long oblong shape that made it seem like a boulevard for parades and a natural slope that enhanced the dramatic impact of buildings. In the mid-1920s, a number of big entrepreneurs clearly realized this and chose this site for commercial buildings. The best examples are the Baťa, Lindt and Stybl companies, whose offices were all designed and built by Ludvík Kysela; Pavel Janák's Hotel Juliš, and Jaromír Krejcar's Olympic Building, this last being an astonishingly precocious example of modern architecture in the very heart of the city. Krejcar – "beauty in modern times resides in mathematics and science" – used reinforced concrete in order to create a facade reduced to pure geometric shapes bare of all decoration. In his first drawings, the facade was smooth, like a giant cinema screen on which advertising would be fixed or projected – modern architecture combining function and propaganda.

The Lindt Building is similarly surprising for a historic city center. The onlooker's first impression on seeing the glass facade is one of luxury because of the material used and then of order because we can see inside.[27] At the same time we cannot miss the advertisements in rows right across the facade and that are fully integrated into the design of the building, an innovation in displaying a company's brand name architecturally. The onlooker might feel some sense of embarrassment at the lack of privacy afforded by the glass elevation, and perhaps also worried by the slenderness of the concrete frame, yet in the end the traditional concrete foundation, conventional rows of floors almost all resembling one another and rooftop gallery are reassuring enough. Here Kysela and Janák, designing a new type of commercial building, were faced with a similar challenge to that of Sullivan in Chicago when he designed the elevations of the first American skyscrapers. Devising a type of functional architecture rekindles the issue of form, and the strict rules of a new aesthetic have to be worked out. This also applies to the shape of the ground plan and to the building's relationship to the city, as we shall see. Kysela was very much at the heart of a contemporary debate: how was Prague to be turned into a capital city? It was his belief that "transforming the big city centers of America and Europe is the number one problem in city planning in modern times.[28] The architect of the Lindt Building, just like the Olympic's Krejcar, argued that the static concept of public spaces was out of date and regretted that the enclosed spaces of ancient cities could not cater for modern man's needs. And whereas Prague had an almost mythic dimension as a large city, in fact it was seriously impaired by the narrowness of the streets, which could not cope with modern traffic. And the fact that so many of the building plots were long thin irregular strips of land perpendicular to the street was in no way conducive to orderly reconstruction, or convenient for pedestrians and shoppers. How could Kysela cater for contemporary needs and resolve that problem? There was in fact a type of construction that got round some of the obstacles, and that was the covered shopping arcade that had been so successful in Paris and certain other cities, appealing to the imagination of writers and idle strollers. Buildings and cities had to coexist in osmosis... An ancient and modest plot of land thus became a stimulus to an imaginative and poetic creation of a place. The edifice was built within the constraints of the site: Kysela removed the boundaries between building and public space, the street, by designing a ground-floor arcade to run through the site from the front to the back of the building. There are numerous pedestrians; the arcade is wide. The city is full of life; the artistic avant-garde is fascinated by images, so the arcade contains a cinema, the first sign of modernity. Czechoslovakia is one of the most industrialized countries in Europe: the interior volumes crowned with concrete beams and glass panels, and the delicate metal-structured frontages are appropriately bold architectural features. Load-bearing steel columns are also used, as in the Ara store. Finally, mention must be made of two later buildings, on the margins of the city center: the House of the Czechoslovakian Union, Dilo, and the department store Bílá Labuť. Both put a final touch to the transparent-facade debate: the metal doors, windows and frames are the essential structure and the cloak of glass both reflects the city and reveals what is happening within.

And so this functional and commercial architecture was one of the prime factors in the transformation of Prague, which was a major event during these inter-war decades.

Baťa and Lindt Buildings

Movement, rhythm, electric power, the wild confusion of New York styles, Broadway by night, these are the things that fascinate the new generation: jazz is all the rage, cinemas are everywhere; Prague has become a city of the night, shimmering with neon advertisements.

GALERIE

Hotel Juliš

1928-1933.
Architect: Pavel Janák.

Bank (former Ara department store)

1927-1931.
Architects: Milan Babuška
and František Řehák.

Opposite page:

House of the Czechoslovakian Union (Dilo)

1934-1938.
Architects: Oldřich Starý
and František Zelenka.
The predominantly glass facade
was used for displaying works of art.

Bílá Labuť department store

1937-1939.
Architects: Josef Hrubý and Josef Kittrich.
A project of modest proportions,
but including the latest technology
(pneumatic tubes, lifts and escalators).

Opposite page and below:

Hôtel Juliš

Interior of the restaurant,
1928-1933. Pavel Janák.

Gallery of the Black Rose

1928-1932.
Architect: Oldřich Tyl.
The concrete ceiling inlaid with round glass
panels filters light down to the two levels
of passageways and the vast shopping area.

Social Insurance Fund Building

also known as the Trades Union Building or
the "general institute of pensions," 1929-1934,
Josef Havlíček and Karel Honzík.
Situated in the Žižkov industrial area, it was
considered Prague's first skyscraper (the
equivalent of thirteen stories high).

Exhibition Center

1924-1928
Josef Fuchs and Oldřich Tyl,
(Refurbished by M. Mazák and associates 1985-94
to house the National Museum of Modern Art).

Social Insurance Fund Building

Ground plan,
Josef Havlíček and Karel Honzík, 1929-1934.

Plan for regulating the Letná Plain

Architect: Josef Gočár, 1937.

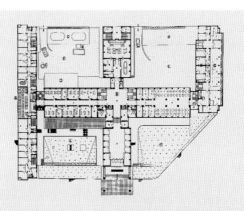 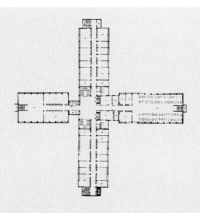 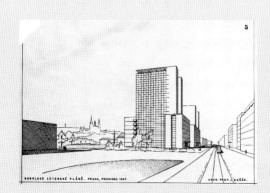

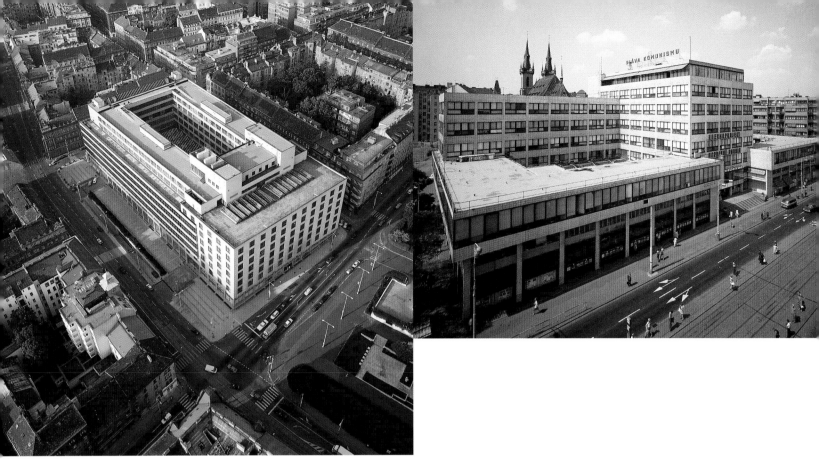

THE MAKING OF
A CAPITAL

Exhibition Center

View from the air, 1924-1928,
Josef Fuchs and Oldřich Tyl, this building
brings a metropolitan scale to Prague.

Top right:

**Administrative building
of the National Electricity Company**

View from the air.
Architects: Adolf Benš and Josef Křiž,
1926-1935.
One of the first buildings in Prague
to have American-style air-conditioning.

The newly fledged capital could not break with its muchadmired Gothic and baroque heritage, nor renege on its ambition to reclaim a leading role in modern Europe. And so what could be more impressive than architecture as a visible demonstration of cultural and technical skills to advertise the political and economic strength of a nation and the aspirations and successes of its people? Masaryk was wise enough to realize the importance of endowing Prague with the appropriate facilities and public buildings. Planners and architects set about enhancing the city's image with ambitious buildings of considerable scale. In an article published in French on the subject of contemporary Czech architecture,[29] Janák expressed the opinion that in the wake of the revolution it was via massive building programs that modern architecture had come to dominate public opinion. For the great buildings that were to be put up in Prague, certain architects such as Gocar, Hübschmann and Janák were in favor of an architecture imbued with the democratic spirit: it should be easy for the public to assimilate and also commemorative, even monumental. Hence we find echoes of classical architecture: a monumental feel created by the sheer size of certain buildings, the rather conventional symmetrical design, and the heavy reliance by certain architects on verticals and horizontals. The dignity and importance of certain buildings lie in the symmetrical design of facades and openings, and the virtues of the state are incarnated in allegorical statuary. In general, it is an architecture that the public can indeed assimilate, if without much enthusiasm. Examples of this are the squat Ministry of Trade and Industry building and the massive Ministry of Czech Railways.[30] Then there is a more modern classical vein opened up by the elegant and sober palace of the Viennese Banking Union. This was followed by:[31] the city library, with an austere travertine facade giving no hint of the luxurious Art Deco interiors; the imposing Ministry of Agriculture; the rather meek Commercial Bank; and the assertive Czech

National Bank. We should also mention in this context the uncompleted design of the Palackého Palace and the surrounding buildings,[32] which freed the perspective toward the towers of the Emmaüs monastery.

There were other tendencies, notably of an avant-garde nature encouraged by the Devětsil Group and personalities such as Honzík and Krejcar. As they saw it, architecture had to reflect above all (but not just) the new organization of society, and thus break with the monumental tradition. The competition for a new parliament building on the empty site of the Letná heights was very revealing in this respect. Most of the designs rejected the monumental concept. This was no doubt due to the political context: the building had to be consistent with the institutional image of the new state, i.e. modern and democratic. Hence the formal sobriety recommended by the young Jaromír Krejcar. Nevertheless, the project proved abortive.

A design that was executed, however, was Fuchs and Tyl's spectacular Exhibition Center. Le Corbusier came to the opening and departed with the waspish verdict: "it's a very grand building, but it's not yet architecture." Grand indeed, and bursting out of its site. As if that were not enough, Tyl intended it to be a far bigger design with a second building identical to the first! Even without the extension, the impact was enormous as the building imposed a metropolitan scale on Prague in comparison with the scale of the historic city. With its mass, sobriety and receding lines, it was designed to be seen from a passing automobile, perhaps anticipating Tyl's vision: "with fast modern transport we can envisage open spaces, star-shaped cross-roads, in keeping with the mood of modern man." It was built in reinforced concrete, and with its rooftop terrace, striking elevations and continuous windows, it brought modern architecture to Prague. The journal *Stavba*, of which Tyl was the editor, made the case for industrialized architecture and the primacy of function. It got what it wanted here.

Not far from this site, the Electricity Supply Building clearly reflected two approaches. While its design kept the internal courtyard or atrium, it nevertheless did not adopt the current monolithic style of the Exhibition Center or certain classical buildings. With its division into three perpendicularly aligned parts, all clearly differentiated as regards size, shape and purpose, it marked a new concept of urban facade. At ground floor level, the alignment along the boundaries of the site is respected, but the differing elevations extend beyond these limits. The client for this project is highly significant. With many buildings equipped with elevators, lighting, domestic appliances etc, the tramway network, and transformers in many places, electricity is a key symbol of modern industrialized Czechoslovakia.

Another piece of representative functionalist architecture was the Social Insurance Fund Building. It was the work of two young men, Havlíček and Honzík, who adopted a cruciform ground plan and wings of different height, extending over the limits of the plot. They consulted Le Corbusier, who approved of their design and included a drawing of his own with his reply. Perhaps his influence can be seen in the fact that the building is raised on piles, thus freeing the ground floor, and in their wish to design similar buildings in the vicinity. Be that as it may, the isolated siting of the building and cruciform design ensured plenty of natural light in the offices and obviated the need for a light well. These architects also worked in another functionalist mode, which gave freer reign to more plastic visual effects while being technically explicit. In their work for the airport at Ruzyne or the Brandejs department store, for example, there are formal borrowings from the esthetics of machines, notably passenger liners and aircraft. The buildings are almost completely in white, with volumes curved like ships' smokestacks or angled like aircraft wings, and there are other thematic details, such as metallic tube railings and portholes.

Finally, in the realm of significant achievements, there is the home of the Mánes Society, designed by Otakar Novotný: situated on the Vltava River between the quayside and an island, it was also a bridge between two currents of the avant-garde, a sophisticated synthesis of the various formal and theoretical schools that were shaking up European architecture.

THE SINGULARITY
OF PLECNIK

The architect Jožě Plečnik moved from Vienna to Prague in 1911: Kotěra, his friend and studio colleague in Otto Wagner's practice, allowed him to take over his teaching post at the College of Decorative Arts. The year 1911, according to Šalda, was the one when new forces arrived, and the pre-war period was rife with polemics in the world of architecture. In Vienna, Plečnik finished the church of the Holy Spirit (in concrete), abandoned the Secession style and turned toward the study of ancient languages.

In 1920, on the advice of Kotěra, who was designing the presidential apartment, Masaryk appointed Plečnik architect for Prague's Hradčany Castle. He stayed in this post until 1935, although often required to be in Ljubljana to fulfill teaching and professional obligations. His pupil, disciple and eventually colleague, Otto Rothmayer, was given the task of supervising the work on a daily basis.[34] At Hradčany the renovation was intended to demonstrate the state's liberation from the Habsburgs. In the words of the president[35]: "the nation regards the castle as an object which belongs to it, so that is why a castle designed for monarchy must be transformed into a democratic castle". So Plečnik interpreted this brief in his own way. He inserted dark paving into the slabs of the first courtyard to create two oblique paths serving new doors, in order to play down the importance of the central door, called the Mathias door, which was a symbol of the Habsburgs. More positively, Plečnik spelled out his intentions by installing items of popular iconography and elements drawn from classical Greek, Roman and Etruscan sources, which were completely accessible to citizens of the times. Individual qualities were exalted by quotations: "We slaves have our own original strength; nevertheless we still have to go often to Rome to find it." The use Plečnik made of small scale effects was consistent with the philosophy of "emotional involvement"[36] of the participants in the experience: regional materials, perfect craftsmanship in the execution of detail, the combining of traditional and modern techniques, all of these were signs and symbols that made interpretation easier, and pointed to the architect's desire to get close to the cultural roots of the inhabitants by means of the work he designed. This was an architecture of dialogue and mutual understanding, consequently democratic. The canopy over the entrance to the staircase of the bull in the southeast corner of the third courtyard is thus an allusion to a regional legend and interprets certain features of Greek architecture without imitating them.

Castle gardens

Hradčany Hill.
In foreground a small belvedere. Saint Nicholas Church in the distance.

Castle gardens

Central part.

Monumental staircase
opening on to Paradise Garden.

Detail of piping
in castle courtyard, 1927-28.

Detail of the Column
Gallery. Air vent, 1927-28.

Opposite page:
The Bull Staircase, 1929-31.

The other ambition of Plečnik was to integrate Hradčany into a proper urban design linking the castle and its immediate surroundings with the city at its foot. The image of the Acropolis dominating the Athens skyline, built in the golden age of Greek democracy, was a powerful precedent.

One of his planned developments was for a cleared route from Wenceslas Square, stretching through Malá Strana and leading up to the castle. In the same spirit, he wanted to integrate the Letná heights into the general plan by providing access routes and designing national projects for a library, theater and military cemetery. These ambitions came to nothing, because Plečnik could not reach an understanding with the planning commission, and he had to be content with minor improvements dotted around the perimeter of the castle. It was obvious at any rate that he wished there to be a solemn pathway of symbolic importance providing vistas and unexpected viewpoints. These were to remind the walker of history, stimulate interest and curiosity, and focus a fresh and revitalizing gaze on existing architecture. While this work was going on, Plečnik designed his other great achievement in Prague, the church of the Sacred Heart. He had the outline of the primitive Christian basilica to work on, with its single nave and no load-bearing point. Between the nave and the main entrance he added a free-standing bell tower to the body of the building. The internal peripheral walls he enlivened with pilasters, and he brought out the asceticism of the holy place by extensive use of bare brick. On the outside he clad the church in a cloak of brown brick decorated with a grid of protruding gray granite blocks. He did not make the structural framework very obvious, but did not try to hide it either: it was the same as the decorative material, either carved or extruded from its mass.

During his time in Prague,[37] Plečnik was a somewhat isolated figure, apart from his friendships with Gočár, Janák and Kotěra and the admiration he inspired in his students. He was a reserved man, more religious in character than a socialite, and in time he developed an atypical architecture that left him more and more marginalized. The avant-garde criticized it for being excessively historical in its references, while conservatives judged it to be too idiosyncratic... Today his work arouses great interest on the part of Czech historians, and it was recently the subject of a superb exhibition,[38] appropriately in Prague Castle.

Entrance to the Presidential Suite,
1923-24.

Detail of staircase leading to Presidential Suite,
1923-24.

The Gold Room,
1924.

Entrance to the Spanish Room,
Otto Rothmayer, 1950-1956.

Column Gallery,
Jože Plečnik, 1927-1930.

Fountain of the Lion Room,
Jože Plečnik, 1923-1924

Detail of the entrance
to the Spanish Room,
completed by Otto Rothmayer,
after Plečnik's death.

Reconstruction of Terezian Wing,
the oldest part of the castle,
by Otto Rothmayer, 1930-1931.

The Evžen Linhart villa

Architect: Evžen Linhart, 1927-1929.

Villa

Front elevation,
Architect: Hana Kučerová, 1932.

Villa

Side elevation,
architect: Hana Kučerová, 1932.

NOTHING IS MORE FATAL
THAN THE ROUTINE OF OUTDATED PLANS…[59]
RAYMOND UNWIN

During the 1920s, the growth of the middle classes and the emergence of a new forward-looking intelligentsia made the private house a prestigious possession. In collaboration with building cooperatives, the government encouraged housing programs right up till the economic crisis of the 1930s. Far out from the city center there were even "garden cities" on a considerable scale (Ořechovka, Hřebenky, Hanspaulka), as well as more modest ones (Spořilov, Zahradní Město).[39] New residential districts were designed, which Janák saw as the real way forward for Prague, as opposed to the ever more intensive and crowded development of the city as it was. The private housing program was consistent with the mood of national emancipation, responding to changing lifestyles, heralding a new civilization and contributing to the dynamism of the city. The private house even began to be associated with a whole art de vivre,[40] and the ideal house in the suburbs ought to resemble, in Šalda 's words, "a beautiful, well-constructed phrase that develops of its own accord."

We have already noticed that some pre-war houses were architecturally progressive in a rationalist way and that Kotěra was the precursor of this trend. We need only think of his own villa, or Sucharda's, in which the building material takes precedence over decoration, and volume dictates spatial organization. While vernacular art was the inspiration behind shapes and colors, it was on English house design that the new culture of the domestic habitat was based.[41] The interior layout corresponded to the needs of the inhabitants and no longer just with the rules of geometry.

There was a return to the 1920s. In avant-garde circles there was intense debate about the family house. The "Pure Four" (Jaroslav Frágner, Karel Honzík, Evžen Linhart, Vít Obrtel) developed a conception of the house that depended entirely on a "scientific analysis of the basic functions." Honzík stressed the need for research, as "nothing is more fatal than the routine of outdated plans."[42] The generation of young architects wanted nothing but functional houses coming off a production line in the manner of American houses (complete with fitted appliances). Implicitly, what was being aimed at was a democratic society. In 1928, the Czechoslovakian Society of Guilds pressed for the building of Dejvice-Baba, a model development that called on three generations

Dejvice-Baba

1928-1934. The overall plan drawn up by Pavel Janák on a grid pattern.

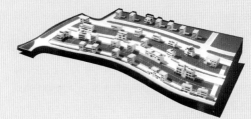

Villa Palička

1929-1932.
Mart Stam, a Dutch architect and the only foreigner involved in the design and building of the Baba district.

Villa Lida Baaroví

(housing two families)
1937, Ladislav Žák.

of architects. On the slope of a hill, Janák designed the estate with the detached villas arranged in rows in such a way that each villa would have a view over Prague through the gap between the two villas in the row beneath. The upper level was at street level where the entrance was situated, whereas the front opened onto a garden and commanded the view. The houses were built only when a design was individually selected by a client, a method of commissioning that distinguished the Dejvice-Baba project from the Weissenhof project in Stuttgart and the Werkbund later in Vienna. Thirty-three houses were built, and were so varied in style and quality that it would be pointless to try to describe them here. A few common denominators can be mentioned nevertheless: distinct or interconnecting volumes, varying treatment of doors and windows in relation to distribution and purpose, projecting balconies and canopies, tiered terraces, flat roofs, monochrome facades, often white. A common feature too was the open plan design and the minimal decorative style (no ornamentation and standard wash rendering). Finally, a sign of the new standards of comfort, use of the latest materials, highquality appliances and contemporary furniture.

These villas, however, were the prerogative of a small minority, mostly in intellectual and artistic circles. The avant-garde project remained unfinished: "When we went on and on about the wonders of modern architecture, which was purely functional and devoid of decoration, and which was aimed at catering for human needs regardless of social class, we didn't anticipate that the outcome of such a difficult battle would apply to just a few privileged people. We didn't anticipate that that white architecture would be just a drop in a black ocean of suffering"... Could this modernity have a future?

Finally, homage should be paid to Adolf Loos, whose theoretical advances fed architectural debate for nearly a quarter of a century. Prague gave him the opportunity to create one of his major works, the Villa Müller in the Střešovice district, which was built between 1928 and 1930. Loos made of it a brilliant demonstration of "Raumplan", literally "space plan" The design of the villa revolves around the interconnection of different floor levels and the space they relate to, resulting in an "architecture of staircases", an architecture that is compact and complex, and can only be appreciated in situ.

Villa Müller

1928-1930. Adolf Loos.
Below: Interior.
Refined decorative style
combined with sumptuous materials.
Right: exterior.

Bank of Bohemia Building

(Zemská Bank)
1936-1937, Richard Ferdinand Podzemný.
Reinforced concrete construction
permitting large glass walls and bays.
(Building known as the "glass palace").

During the 1930s, big building projects came to an end and the economic crisis loomed up on the horizon. This time, the avant-garde dreams of working on full-scale projects for the people coincided with contemporary needs: in reaction to capitalist society, local authority housing became a new priority and was supported by building cooperatives that helped with the financing. As a direct consequence of the economic crisis, the maximum surface of a subsidized apartment went down in 1930 from 288 sqare feet to 144, and then from 144 to 123. On this basis, the new regulations defined the concept of "minimal accommodation," consisting of one room (doubling as dining room and bedroom) and a kitchen, and a WC lit and ventilated on the outside wall.

With community housing and ideological commitment being allied, the matter of style became secondary, and functional architecture was the order of the day. In the view of Teige, "the society of the future must be prepared for, architecture must be revolutionized." Community housing could not be characterized by class distinction but had to be conceived on the democratic basis of equal accommodation for everyone, calculated in terms of the amount of individual space allocated to an adult. In Teige's words, "the architectural avant-garde for whom flat roofs or metallic furniture were not the main aim or desir has discovered the link between housing and the economic and social crisis. This avant-garde working for the idea of social progress must be politically committed." In fact Teige published a work entitled *Architecture and the Class Struggle* and launched the watchword for the times: community housing. In 1929, Devětsil put an end to its existence and was replaced by the Left Front. The Czech avant-garde grew in importance on the strength of its political commitment. At the third congress of the CIAM in 1930, the Czechoslovakian delegation put forward plans for a new type of accommodation, the Communal House, a complex of private residential "cells" and shared facilities. In the competition organized by the central office for social insurance, the "L" (Left Front in Czech) Project proposed an individual cell of 35 square feet. This space might seem prison-like out of the context of the whole project, which related minimal personal space to generous communal allocations. The Communal House project should in fact be interpreted as an urban project organizing a whole city and coordinating social activities on a neighborhood or quarter basis. The Formula combined a new scale of building with a more democratic political order, providing a fresh stimulus to modernity in architecture.

For his part, Teige also tried to optimize the "minimal accommodation". He relied heavily on the principle of the railway-sleeping compartment, a volume of space determined by a fixed number of occupants and their specific requirements, yet allowing a degree of modern comfort. His proposal was for a cell of between 32 and 72 square feet (depending on intended use) and including technical innovations to make the best use of space at particular times of the day (fold-away beds and furniture that could be stacked or folded, etc). There were also architectural ploys to create a greater impression of space (large bay windows, and sliding doors and windows). With its guiding principle of the equal accommodation for everyone, the avant-garde met with a favorable reception and was given commissions. Their success was not always as enthusiastically acclaimed by the public as by the authorities, as "minimal accommodation" was still insecure (in 1936, when the last big competition took place, the theme was "Houses for the Poor" – terms originating in the law).

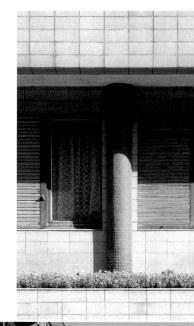

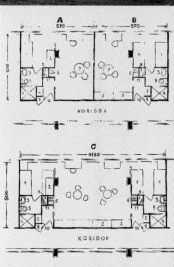

Above and top right:
Apartment block
Josef Havliček.
Staircase and detail of facade.

Above:
Social housing apartment block.
Architect: František Maria Černy
and Karel Ossendorf, 1930-1937.

Plans for the Communal House, 1930.
Josef Havlíček and Karel Honzík.
Submitted to CIAM.
Right: plan of "cell" accommodation unit.
Opposite page, below: scale model.

In the final reckoning these designs had a decisive impact on contemporary local authority housing and for some time to come, as well as on the private rented sector even with a high level of comfort. This last point can be illustrated by the example of the Podzemný Building. It was an amalgamation of a number of plots producing almost 275 yards of frontage on the northern fringe of Letná. This was highcost land in a prestigious neighborhood, which was a cause for concern among democrats opposed to any social distinction. Although the block contains luxury apartments with conservatories, it also has communal facilities (roof gardens, basement garages and shops). The original plan even contained a tennis court and a games area, which, although hardly workers' activities, were at least communal. The block also reflects contemporary debates about health and preventive medicine, as there was a move at the time to get more light into apartments. As this development had sufficient mass, it would have been an obvious solution to have central courtyards for services and deliveries. Instead, however, of this, the apartments were designed to run through from the front to the back of the building, with an en bloc layout more in the contemporary style, which preferred isolated volumes to the urban continuum, if not the linearity of Haussmann to the townhouse, and the boulevard to the street.

On the other hand, a lot of private rented apartments were built on high-density in-fill sites in or near the city center. In these constricted developments the apartments were designed on the through-plan to get the maximum light. The central area contained the entrance (the traditional nineteenthcentury system), and some indirect light came through glass-paneled doors and partitions. The problem of light was not an easy one to solve and often imposed constraints on the design and layout of accommodation.

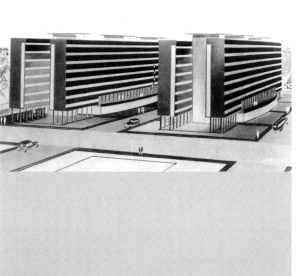

Above:
Social housing apartments.
Architects: František Albert Libra and Jiří Kan, 1930-1936.

THE **CZECH** *LANDS* from 1938 to 1948

In 1938, after the annexation of Austria by Nazi Germany, Czechoslovakia was in great peril. Encouraged by Hitler, the ethnic German minority at first demanded autonomy and then annexation by the Third Reich. The Czechs were ready to defend themselves, and the inhabitants of Prague demonstrated en masse to demand that the government resist German claims. But they were abandoned by their principal ally, France, which was intent on avoiding war at all costs. On September 29, 1938, Great Britain, Germany, Italy and France signed the Munich Pact ceding to Germany those Czech territories populated by more than 50 percent ethnic Germans. In 1939, Hitler delivered the coup de grace to what remained of Czechoslovakia. On March 14, Slovakia proclaimed its independence, and the next day German troops occupied Prague to establish the Protectorate of Bohemia and Moravia. For just over six years, the swastika was to fly over Prague.

Hitler thus got his hands on the enormous industrial power of Bohemia, especially the Skoda armaments factories, which were among the most modern in Europe. Hence the relatively favorable treatment reserved for the Czech population for the time being: Germany needed the industry and the manpower that went with it. Any resistance was brutally suppressed. After the student demonstrations of October and November 1939, the Nazis sentenced nine students to death by firing squad, sent another 1,200 to concentration camps, and closed the universities and elite training institutions. Prague had to get used to the sight of public notices in German, Nazi military parades and propaganda, anniversary celebrations for the Führer, anti-Semitic legislation (compulsory wearing of the yellow star after September 1, 1940) and Gestapo terror. More than 3,000 Prague inhabitants were shot, hanged or guillotined.

In September 1941, the fearsome SS leader Reinhard Heydrich arrived in Prague to be in charge of the Protectorate, and arrests and executions increased. In November 1941, the fortress town of Terezin, 40 miles from Prague, was turned into a ghetto. Of the 39,395 Prague Jews who were sent there, 31,709 were murdered in extermination camps.

On May 27, 1942, two Czech parachutists, sent by the Czech government in exile in England to relaunch the internal resistance, fatally wounded Heydrich. The Nazis proclaimed martial law and unleashed a reign of terror. They shot hostages and completely wiped out the village of Lidice near Prague: the men were shot and women and children sent to concentration camps, and the houses were burned to the ground. On July 3, the authorities of the Protectorate held a giant rally of support for the Reich in Wenceslas Square, which was allegedly attended by 250,000 people.

From 1944 on, Prague was the target for Anglo-American bombing raids that killed more than 1,000 people. On May 5, 1945, when American troops were at Plzeň, less than 65 miles from Prague, there was an uprising in the city, but the Americans respected the agreement made with the Soviet Union and did not intervene. Faced with German soldiers determined to fight, the Czechs received help

from an unexpected source, the army of General Vlassov. This consisted of anti-Communist Russians who had fought with the Nazis and who now hoped to escape the clutches of their compatriots by turning on the Germans and gaining the favor of the Americans. The Red Army entered Prague on May 9, wiped out the last pockets of German resistance and enjoyed the credit for the liberation of Prague. The soldiers of Vlassov's army, meanwhile, were captured by the Americans, handed over to the Russians and promptly sent to the Gulag. The Prague rising led to the deaths of 1,694 inhabitants, and resulted in considerable damage around the National Museum and the Old Town square, where a whole wing of the Town Hall was burned down.

In 1943, the Beneš government in exile in London had signed an agreement to cooperate with the Soviet Union. It was obvious that, after the defection of the Western allies in 1938, newly liberated Czechoslovakia's destiny would be more closely bound up with that of the Soviet Union. Negotiations between the London exiles and those in Moscow culminated in the creation of the National Front, to which were admitted only those parties that had fought against Nazism. President Beneš returned to Prague on May 16, 1945. On October 25, he chose the moment of a rally in Wenceslas Square to announce the nationalization of the banks, insurance companies, coalmines, heavy industry and the foodprocessing industry. In the 1946 elections, the last free ones before 1990, Communist candidates received more than 40 percent of the votes in Bohemia and Moravia. Their leader, Klement Gottwald became prime minister in the coalition government. Gradually Communists took control of the unions, media and security services. The Iron Curtain fell on the country in 1947, when Stalin ruled out any thought of Czechoslovakia being included in the Marshall Plan. The inevitable epilogue came in February 1948: the Communists took skillful advantage of a government crisis caused by non-Communist ministers, threatened intervention by the armed "people's militia" under their control, and effected a total takeover of power. In June, Beneš resigned and Gottwald became president of the republic.

František Gross

Libeň,
c. 1942, National Gallery, Prague.

Vojtěch Preissig

Birth of the Earth,
1936, National Gallery, Prague.

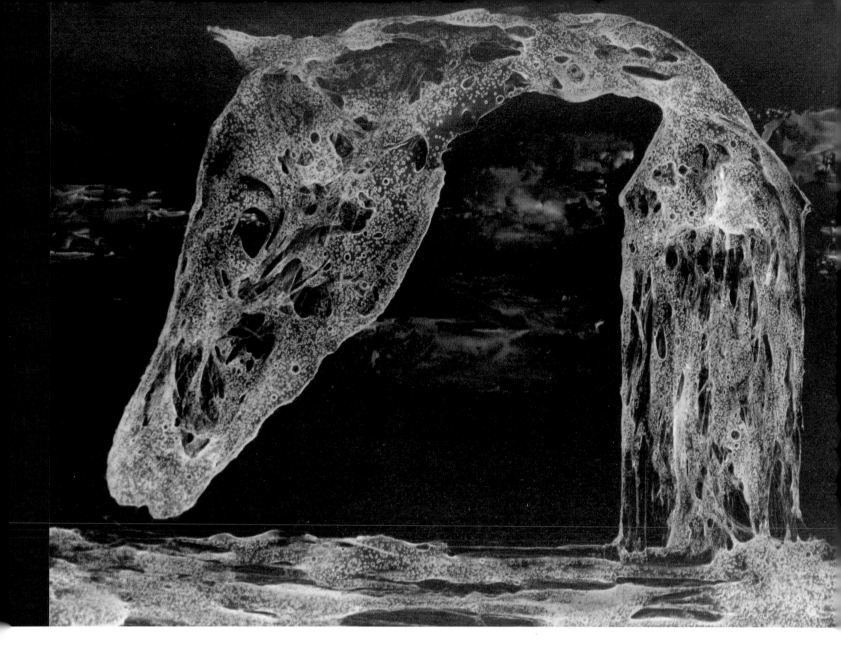

Jindřich Heisler

From the cycle *"Of the Same Flour"*,
1944, photographism, private collection.

CZECH CULTURE
UNDER THE PROTECTORATE

From the moment of the Munich Pact, censorship came into operation. Under German pressure, the minister of the interior canceled the license of the Liberated Theater, which had been very committed to the anti-Nazi struggle. German refugees also found themselves silenced, and many of them emigrated. In 1939, certain artists reacted to the occupation by creating works that protested at the triumph of barbarism, such as Josef Čapek 's cycle *The Fire*. The German occupation took a heavy toll on Czech culture. Artists and writers were arrested and sent to concentration camps, such as Josef Čapek, Emil Filla and Vojtěch Preissig (1873-1944), an abstract painter who came back to Prague in 1930 after twenty years in the United States. Others were executed, such as the novelist Vladislav Vančura, a former member of Devětsil, in 1942.

Yet cultural life did not come to a halt. Painters still had exhibitions, and new groups came into existence, like Group 7 in October, which exhibited from 1939 to 1941, and Group 42. Films were

Photograph from the cycle
"On the Needles of our Days," linking
photographs by Štyrský and poems
by Heisler, 1941.

Alén Divis

Guillotine,
1941 National Gallery, Prague.

Karel Teige

Collage.

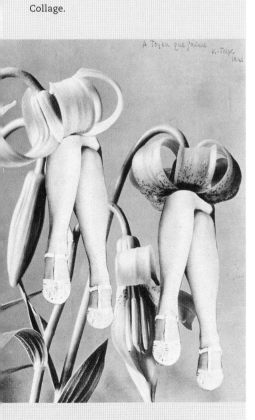

still made, and the Barrandov studios were even expanded by the Nazis. Before the closure of all theaters and places of entertainment in September 1944, theater activity carried on in Prague and was sometimes a form of anti-Nazi resistance. The Burian Theater was also used for exhibitions of painting before Burian was arrested in 1941. The great solitary master of Czech photography, Josef Sudek, hardly set foot outside his door during the whole of the occupation, and began his famous series, "Window of my Studio." In 1946, in the La Boétie Gallery in Paris, an exhibition was held, entitled "Czechoslovakian Art 1938-1946," which was proof enough that cultural life in Prague had not been extinguished during the war.

One of the most important events of the period was the creation of Group 42, the leading members of which were the painters František Gross, František Hudeček, Kamil Lhoták (born in 1912), Ladislav Zívr, the photographer Miroslav Hák, poets such as Jiří Kolář (born in 1912) and critics like Jindřich Chalupecký (1910-1990). Certain members had been associated with Surrealism, and at first the group favored a poetic or magic realism before turning toward the reality of everyday life. If the group had a manifesto, it was perhaps Chalupecký 's essay, published in 1940, and entitled "The World in Which" We Live. Here he argued that for a modern painter or poet, "reality is identified with the city, with its inhabitants, streets, lampposts, signs and notices, blocks of flats, staircases, apartments." He considered it necessary to "reflect on the poetic value of modern life. " In the same vein, the Group 42 painters devoted themselves to the theme of man's (often tragic) destiny in the face of the ever-difficult reality of daily life. For these painters, Surrealism was no longer on the agenda.

Nevertheless, it is far from the case that Surrealism had disappeared from Prague. The Surrealist group went clandestine in 1939, keeping active and productive throughout the war. A new member had joined them in 1938, Jindřich Heisler (1914-1953), a friend of Toyen and Štyrský. Heisler, a Jew, was thus doubly clandestine and spent the duration hiding in Toyen's apartment. The three friends published short collections of poems, collages and drawings such as *Only the Rattles Piss Peacefully on the Ten Commandments*. Toyen created the cycles of drawings *Fire* (1939-1940) and *Hide Yourself, War!* (1944). Heisler and Toyen also created poems in the form of photographed three-dimensional objects, which they published clandestinely under the title *The Bunkers of Sleep*. And in 1942, for Toyen's fortieth birthday, Teige and Heisler published an album of collages entitled *Life Begins at Forty*. Other Surrealists, who were not part of the official group, were nevertheless active; in 1942 several members of the future Ra group, such as Josef Istler (born in 1919), illegally published the collection *Dolls in Shreds*.

Paradoxically, the period of the Protectorate was a sort of golden age of Czech Surrealist photography. Heisler was intensely interested in it, and tried to make his photographs as unreal as possible, endlessly experimenting with a very diverse range of techniques. To capture his dreams (which were sometimes nightmares), he wanted images that were both "poetic and haunted". Thus in 1943-1944 he made a cycle entitled *Of the Same Flour* which consisted of "photo-graphics," images of the greatest originality technically and stylistically. They were of white, "floury" textures and figurative subjects on a black background strangely deformed by the effect of acid. They were a testimony to the devastations of war, a shattered landscape inhabited by spectral animals and dematerialized human figures. Heisler also made original objects, intended solely to be photographed.

Václav Zykmund (born in 1914) produced Surrealist plays in apartments in 1944-1945 with the help of other members of the future Ra group and their friends. Wearing mysterious ornaments and signs, the performers were surrounded by Surrealist and symbolic objects; Zykmund turned it into a clandestine work, *The Menacing Compass*.

Funke also reacted to the war with his cycle *The Unsated Earth*: photographs of cemeteries are the setting for the Surrealist theme of civilization's traces being destroyed and absorbed by the universe of vegetation. One photograph shows a human hand bursting out of foliage.

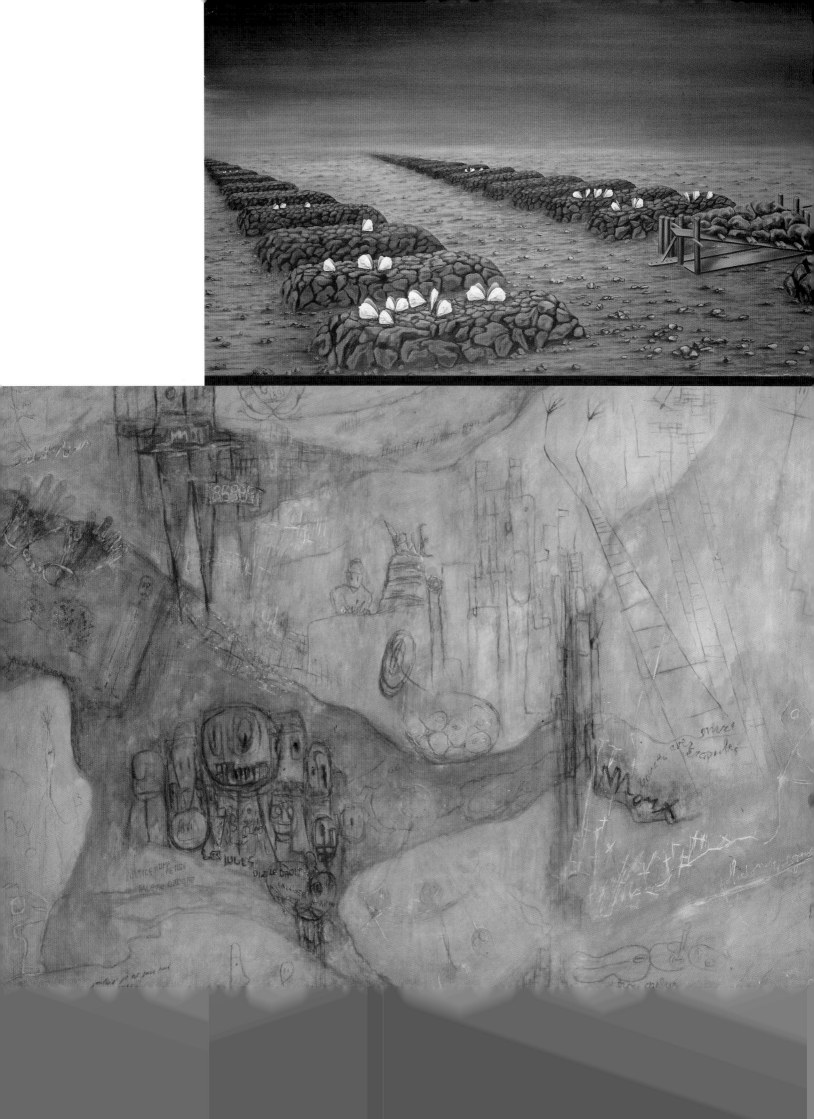

Toyen

Before Spring,
1945, oil on canvas,
Musée national d'art
moderne, Pompidou
Center, Paris.

After the end of the war, artistic activity was intense. A whole series of single exhibitions was devoted to artists who died during the Protectorate, such as Čapek, Preissig, and Štyrský. Big retrospectives were organized from 1946 onwards for Kupka, Šíma and Toyen. In that same year the famous Prague Spring Music Festival was held for the first time.

A number of powerful works were inspired by the war, particularly by members of the future Surrealist group Ra. Václav Tikal (1906-1965) devoted work to the destruction of Lidice en 1942, Bohdan Lacin (born in 1912) painted the Triumph of Death, Václav Zykmund The Hearts of the Dead Swallows, and the photographer Vilém Reichmann (born in 1908) who spent his whole life seeking out fantastic objects and juxtaposing them, between 1945 and 1948 created the cycle *The Wounded City,* an assemblage of silent objects that made up a particularly eloquent denunciation of war.

The clandestine collections of Toyen, Štyrský and Heisler were published. However, even though there was a big Surrealist exhibition in Prague in 1947 (a smaller version of the Paris World's Fair), the Prague group itself was not as active as previously, and that same year Toyen and Heisler went off to Paris for good. A new generation was taking its place. In 1946 the Ra group, which included Josef Istler, Vilém Reichmann, Václav Zykmund and Václav Tikal, published its anthology And Whereas the War... The group wanted to continue a in certain Surrealist tradition, while maintaining a critical distance from the first generation. Little by little their painting became more abstract, not objective, but still dream-like and enigmatic in atmosphere.

At the time when jazz was all the rage, Czech artists revived their contacts with foreign artists. In 1946 Prague saw a succession of big exhibitions on French sculpture and painting, modern English art and modern American art. A year later it was the turn of Belgian art, and that same year the Ra group established links with the COBRA movement (Copenhagen, Brussels, Amsterdam) and the revolutionary French, Belgian and Danish Surrealists. At the same time, the outside world was reminded of the rich cultural heritage of the First Republic. In 1947 the tireless Karel Teige wrote the texts for Modern Architecture in Czechoslovakia for the Ministry of Information and Das Moderne Lichtbild in der Tchechoslowakei (Modern Photography in Czechoslovakia), to accompany an exhibition in Zurich and Vienna.

The Czech film industry, which was nationalized in August 1945, was in full swing. In 1947 the FAMU, the national cinema school, was founded in Prague; this was the birthplace of the Czech "new wave" in the 1960s. Czech animation cinema began to make a name for itself abroad. In 1946 Jiří Trnka's *The Gift* was among the prizewinners in Cannes, and a year later the painter Kamil Lhoták's *Atom at the Crossroads* had a similar success at the Venice Biennale. The "Lion d'Or" that same year was awarded to Karel Steklý for The Mermaid, a film adapted from a realist novel with a social theme.

The artists of Group 42 were active until 1948. Their central concern was man's place in the modern world and they anticipated later fashions such as Pop Art and the new figurative style of the sixties in particular.

Alén Divis

Prison Wall,
National Gallery, Prague.

ARCHITECTURE
1938-1948
A FORM OF RESISTANCE

The time of the Munich Pact brought grief to Czechoslovakia, and there was worse to come. There was little scope for architecture in Prague, sandwiched as it was between the megalomania of Albert Speer, planning the deranged visions of the Berlin axis and the grandiloquence of the "Soviet Union" at the time of the competition for the Palace of the Soviets.

Czech intellectuals as a whole formed a "Civic Front" opposing the invader. Resisting the call for art for the people, Teige vigorously defended his concept of functional architecture. Galvanized into action by the ultimate provocation of the German occupation the avant-garde organized an exhibition entitled "For a New Architecture," in 1940. At the inauguration there were several speeches defining architecture as the strongest expression of national culture and stressing its mission of contributing to ethical values. The exhibition itself was a retrospective glorifying architecture in modern Czechoslovakia, the country one and undivided as it was at the time of democracy. The achievements were grouped by type of building – hospitals, schools, etc – to accentuate the firm social values of the past. Books were also exhibited, of the type burned by the Nazis in Berlin... Another symbolic message was that the exhibition was held in Prague Castle and was entered by the luxurious Garden of Paradise laid out by the Slovene Plečnik. In essence it proclaimed the cultural identity of a Czechoslovakian Republic that had gone forever. Once again architecture was mobilized on behalf of democracy and modern civilization, and had to become a form of intellectual resistance. This was a political act that was fraught with danger: there was the precedent of the Nazi persecution of the Bauhaus, that was considered to be anti-German, internationalist and Bolshevik, resulting in it being closed down in 1933.

An inventory of the architectural work completed at this time and an investigation of the archives still has not been carried out. Generally speaking there were few new projects. The National Museum of Techniques, closing off the perspective from the Letná, was completed. Mention should be made too of Havlicek's utopian plans for Charles University. He designed three skyscrapers that

ALL THE SIGNS ARE THAT FREEDOM AND POETRY ARE GOING TO BECOME REALITY.
TEIGE

Design competition in 1946 for rebuilding the Town Hall. Entry submitted by František Maria Černy (First Prize), who sought to reconcile the urban scale and the character of the nineteenthcentury city.

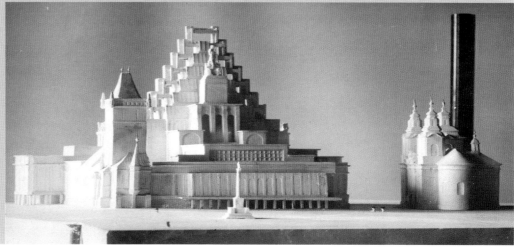

Smíchov Station

1947-1954.
Jan Zázvorka and Jan Zák.

Design competition for
rebuilding the Town Hall.
1910.
Jiři Štursa and Josef Gočár.

would make an impact on the horizon and dreamed of transforming the city of stone into a garden-city. Although the obsolescence of the university buildings and their scattered position made the project seem legitimate, it was in fact quite subversive. At a time when university activities were being censored, this modern architecture was a reminder of the former prestige of the capital; and when the walls of Havlíček and Honzík 's Social Insurance Fund Building (1929) were painted green to camouflage them from Allied air raids, the architect put up ostentatious towers.

As soon as peace came, it was time to take stock. The city had not suffered from much bombing. But one notable hit was in the Old City, where the neo-Gothic wing of the Town Hall was destroyed. A competition was held for designing its reconstruction and extending the administrative center, and the opportunity was taken to pull down the nineteenthcentury blocks enclosing the square. Hence the radical nature of certain projects, such as Stursa's. Above all, Prague resumed its status as the capital of Czechoslovakia, and once again – and once again with no decision being taken – a competition was held for designing a parliament building on the Letná plateau. Generally speaking, the upturn in political fortunes was a period when some thought was given to organizing things for the better, defining new priorities in architecture, and reestablishing the republican values that had been those of Czechoslovakia under Masaryk, to create a better future. Thus Teige published what was to be his last work *Modern Architecture in Czechoslovakia*, which was published by the ministry of propaganda in 1947. Significantly for the times, it was published in several languages, and pride of place was given to the front-cover illustration of Krejcar's pavilion for the Paris World's Fair of 1937. Optimism was in the air and Teige felt free to write:[45] "All the signs are that freedom and poetry are going to become reality." This was 1947, a time when there were hopes of a better world, but when it was also possible to hear the first creaking of the Iron Curtain.

PRAGUE

in the nineteen-fifties

In February 1948, a reign of terror and arbitrary power seized control of Czechoslovakia once again. In the "Purge" more than 250,000 people lost their jobs. The new regime cleared out the whole upper echelons of the army, the Police and the Educational profession.

The state funeral of ex-President Beneš in October 1948 was the last expression of protest against the new regime, although the government deployed armed militias to prevent groups of mourners reaching the capital from the provinces. Immediately thereafter, the Communist leadership of the country adopted a hard line. Labor camps were set up, with the worst fate being that of people who were sent to the uranium mines. So-called "enemies of the regime" were dealt with in show trials: leaders of the non-Communist parties, Slovak "bourgeois nationalists", organizers of internal resistance, Czechs who had fought in England with the Allies, religious leaders, clerics, "agents of the Vatican" and others.

It is estimated that at least 230,000 people were victims of rigged trials; of 232 death sentences, 178 were carried out. Once all opposition was wiped out, it then became the turn even of some Communist leaders themselves, beginning with those who had fought in the Spanish Civil War. In 1952, eleven leaders were hanged, including Rudolf Slánský, the ex-secretary of the Communist Party, a victim of the process that he himself had initiated.

The citizens of Prague lived once again as they had during the Nazi Protectorate: in a climate of fear, betrayal and victimization; incredibly, there was even a resurgence of anti-Semitism at the time of the Slánský trial. Propaganda came into every sphere of life. There were parades and mass rallies, and the May Day celebrations replaced the Führer's birthday. Pictures of Stalin supplanted those of Hitler; and allegiance to the Third Reich gave way to expressions of loyalty to the Soviet Union. The difference this time was that there were intellectuals capable of applauding the hanging of "traitors"... Most of the population, intellectuals included, kept quiet.

The Stalin Monument

Otakar Švec

The essence of socialist realism, representing the Czech and Soviet nations being led by Stalin toward a radiant future. The 14,000 ton monument was built in 1955 and was produced by 600 workers out of 7,000 cubic meters of granite. Otakar Švec, a very good artist of the 1920s, took his life before the inauguration, at a time when the Stalin cult was at its peak. In October 1956, at the 20th congress of the Soviet Communist Party, the personality cult was denounced and with it the monument to Stalin. It was dynamited secretly in 1962.

VELIKÝ STALIN

Above:
An artist long since forgotten shows President Klement Gottwald (first president after the putsch of February 28, 1948) looking confidently toward the "radiant Socialist future," surrounded by workers.

Above right:

"The Great Stalin"

The poster and paintings of the 1950s are characteristic of Socialist Realism, glorifying labor, contemporary political figures and the Socialist revolution.

The only certain way to escape the Communist terror was to go into exile, and more than 25,000 people left Czechoslovakia between 1948 and 1951. Daily life was difficult, and the 1950s was a time of intense gloom. The whole social and economic structure of the past was shattered. The regime banned and then dissolved the Sokols, the nationalist sporting organization created in the nineteeth century that had contributed so much to the social fabric of Czech life. The press, radio and television (the latter first appearing in 1953) were entirely in the hands of the Communist Party. One after another, private firms were nationalized, including small ones, and trade came under the control of the state; agriculture was collectivized. Foreign trade was entirely directed toward the Soviet Union and the rest of the Eastern bloc, and Czechoslovakia, with its relatively advanced economy, found itself absorbed within a virtually under-developed area. The shortage of basic supplies and the devaluation of the currency caused considerable discontent, culminating in June 1953 in a workers' rising in Plzeň, the bastion of heavy industry. Three months earlier, the first "working class president" of Czechoslovakia met with a Surrealistic fate: he caught a chill at Stalin's funeral and died a few days later.

The Khrushchev's denunciation of the "personality cult" and of Stalin's crimes in 1956 caused considerable embarrassment for the Czechoslovakian Communist Party, but it did not change its line. Only writers deplored the general climate of stagnation, at the second Writers's Union Congress in April 1956. The poet Jaroslav Seifert, a former Devětsil member, criticized writers for having failed in their traditional mission of being the "conscience of the nation". Writers denounced their docile stance, their silence during Stalin's crimes, and made a demand for creative freedom. This surge of restlessness caused a thaw that permitted a slight freeing of the limits on cultural expression. But the party would not change, and in 1959 freedom of expression in Czech cultural life was put back into chains.

After February 1948, artists' independent associations were dissolved and their magazines ceased to appear. Artists and intellectuals were surprised by the increasing authoritarianism of the new regime, especially as many of them had been on the left before the war and in some cases were even party members. In this climate, Group 42 and Ra went out of existence. The following year a centralized organization was created called the Czechoslovakian Artists' Union (by analogy with the Architects' Union , Writers' Union, etc). Its purpose was to control the activities of artists, impose ideological correctness, supervise and check on exhibitions, allocate studios, and award public commissions. At the same time, part of the country's artistic heritage was hidden away, in particular Cubism, Surrealism and abstract art. Contacts with the West were brutally severed. A number of artists submitted to this control, others engaged in a kind of passive resistance or worked in isolation. For those who wanted to get away from the official shackles of "serious" art, there were a few creative havens that were less ideologically regimented, such as children's book illustration, cartoon cinema and marionette theater.

The number one ideologist of the new regime was Zdeněk Nejedlý, the minister of education, science and the arts, who was seventy years old in 1948 and had published a book in 1946 entitled *The Communists, Heirs of the Great Traditions of the Czech People*. This former student of Masaryk invented a curious cocktail of Marxism, Socialist Realism, Pan-Slavism and traditional Czech culture. His main theme was the "hunt for traditions" in the "camp of popular democracy". In the Czech past he found them on the one hand in the saga of Jan Hus, for which he suggested a social re-reading, and on the other in nineteenthcentury culture devoted to nationalist themes. He thus created a cult of the author of historical novels and short stories, Alois Jirásek, and the painter Mikuláš Aleš. His ideas went hand in hand with a policy of restoring national monuments; the regime went so far as to build a replica of the Chapel of Bethlehem, in the Old City, where Jan Hus had spread the Word.

The Socialist Realist doctrine took hold very quickly and there was a profusion of poems singing the glory of Stalin and the heroic soldiers of the Red Army, novels about building Socialism and the enthusiastic labors of workers making the society of the future.

The "master-piece" of Socialist Realism in Prague, the absolute symbol of this period, disappeared in 1962. It was a gigantic monument to the glory of Stalin situated on Letná, the hill that overlooks the city. Six hundred workers had labored nonstop for a year and a half to erect this 98-foot statue weighing 14,000 tons. The monument depicted the Czechoslovakian people (a worker, a peasant woman, an "intellectual worker" and a soldier) together with four similar Soviet Russian figures, all being guided toward Communism by Joseph Stalin.

The author of the work, the sculptor Otaka Švec, who had made the famous *Motorcyclist* in the 1920s, committed suicide before his work was inaugurated on May 1, 1955.

Despite this appalling situation, Czech art managed to survive, notably that current of it that seemed so profoundly in tune with the "Czech soul", Surrealism. Although after February 1948 any public Surrealist creation was impossible, the movement went underground for the second time and a whole group of younger poets and artists regrouped semi-illegally around Karel Teige. They included Vratislav Effenberger, Karel Hynek, Josef Istler, Jan Kotík, Zdeněk Lorenc, Mikuláš Medek and Emila Medková. In 1951, they managed to produce a series of ten bulletins for private distri-

Toyen
Trail in the Mirror,
oil on canvas, 1959, Musée national
d'art moderne, Pompidou Center, Paris.

bution, entitled *The Signs of the Zodiac*, consisting of typed texts and reproductions of photographs. Teige died that same year, and Vratislav Effenberger (1923-1986) took over his role as the group's theoretician. Between 1952 and 1962, a series of five anthologies were produced, entitled *Object* and numbered 1 to 5. It was during the dark days of Stalinism, between 1948 and 1953, that Emila Medková (1928-1985) began to photograph arrangements of Surrealist objects. In most of them one finds glass eyes, an obvious symbolic reference to the climate of surveillance and suspicion during the new regime. She abandoned this theme and sought fantastic non-figurative shapes in the reality of urban civilization.

Even before the writers raised their voices in protest, the students of the Academy of Fine Arts were active. In December 1954, they denounced the stagnant cultural climate by organizing Dadaist-type happenings with musicians from the Academy of Music, and did the same in 1956 and 1957. They included artists who are now famous, Bedřich Dlouhý (born in 1932), the sculptor Karel Nepraš (born in 1932) and Jaroslav Vožniak (born in 1933), who in 1957 created the Šmidrové Group, and worked most of the time in the grotesque vein. The title was taken from the name of the policeman character in marionette theater. The continuity of Czech art was maintained in this way, in a very different tradition from Socialist Realism.

The thaw in artistic matters came in fact in that year, 1957. An exhibition entitled "The Founders of Modern Czech Art" allowed the public to see the work of the Cubo-Expressionist generation that had been hidden away. At the same time, as well as the work of the Šmidrové Group, there were other

Stanislav Podhrazsky
Coat,
Bronze, 1948,
National Gallery, Prague.

groups of young artists who had come along since 1948, "May 57" and "Itinerary". Jan Kotík, who had once belonged to Group 42, managed to have an exhibition of his abstract work. *Rudé Právo*, the very official and very dogmatic daily newspaper of the party, denounced "an art that is soulless and empty, made for snobs, blasé gourmets… a sterile flower of the degenerate bourgeois world."

Nevertheless, perhaps in reaction against the officially approved realism, an introspective type of abstraction firmly took root in the Prague artistic landscape of the 1950s. Although it hardly corresponded with a fashion, as the artists in question were almost completely cut off from the outside world, there was something profoundly Czech about this form. It had some of its roots in Surrealism, but also inherited an interest in the spiritualization of matter from the baroque tradition.

In 1958, these young groups were able to exhibit in Prague, and another group came into being, UB 12 which included artists who were to go on to become leaders figures in Czech art of our time, Václav Boštík, Vladimír Janoušek, Věra Janoušková, Stanislav Kolíbal, Alena Kučerová, Adriena Šimotová, Jiří John (1923-1972), and which exhibited for the first time in 1962. The gallery called The Czechoslovakian Writer even held a retrospective of the work of the Surrealist painter Václav Tikal (1906-1965).

This artistic ferment often came into conflict with the dogmatic Communist leaders. The exhibition of Jiří Balcar's (1929-1968) action painting, which had been authorized by the Artists' Union in 1959, was strongly criticized by *Rudé Pravo*: "Repulsive abstractavist junk, kitsch canvases meaninglessly sprayed with all sorts of colours". That same year, statues by Eva Kmentová and Olbram Zoubek were removed from an exhibition of the "Itinerary" group because they were allegedly "an offense to human dignity."

The thaw also affected the theater: 1958 was the year when two little theaters were founded, Balustrade and Semaphore, which tried to revive the pre-war Prague tradition and had a big role to play in the resurgence of cultural life in the city in the 1960s.

Zbynek Sekal

Dead Head,
Bronze, 1957,
National Gallery, Prague.

Hôtel Yalta

1954-1956.
Antonín Tenzer,
designer of the interior.

Opposite page:

**New Tower
of the Emmaus Church**

1959-1968.
František Maria Černý
and Vladimir Kamberský.
Vyšehradská 49.
After being damaged
in the Anglo-American
bombing of 1945,
the decapitated church
was covered with a double
roofing in reinforced
concrete.

After the Communist putsch, the avant-garde was weakened by the break-up of associations, disappearance of journals and general climate of fear. There was a kind of precarious freedom for a while, enlivened by visits from French architects such as Auguste Perret, who had nothing but praise for Prague's baroque heritage as well as the modern buildings of Zlín (the town built by the Baťa shoe company). However, the time when Teige could liken Prague to one of the intellectual and political centers of Europe had gone forever. He himself could no longer publish and was not to survive these dark hours, soon falling victim to a heart attack. The avant-garde mourned its mentor. Prague was suffocating under the lead weight of oppression.

From the start, the regime drew up quinquennial plans for the restructuring of industry and reconstruction of the country.[46] The priority in city planning was to build a high number of dwellings as well as whole new towns.[47] Architecturally this meant standardization of design and industrialization, especially at the very beginning of the 1960s; there was little scope for innovation.

As a result of all the nationalizations, private architectural practices went out of business. Architects became state civil servants working for the Stavoprojekt Institute, which is where a lot of the big names of the former avant-garde ended up. Although their room for individual maneuver was seriously impaired, many made the best of this status, which allowed them to organize the profession, set up teams, even retain something of their former studio setup. On the other hand they were subject to propaganda, which denigrated the esthetes of Purism and Functionalism and recommended a so-called "official" style. This seemed difficult to impose, nevertheless, because its architectural parameters remained vague, as we see from the International Hotel, a mixture of Muscovite symbol and American skyscraper.

In the event, the question of style was of little importance at a time when building operations in the city center were few and far between, and just a number of housing projects were completed on the periphery. These were solid, low-rise blocks of spartan apartments with plain elevations, like the Solidarita estate. One of the few public displays was the Stalin's statue, which was situated along the noble axis of the Old City, with the Letná hill as its natural base and an enormous stone pedestal. It was an irony of history that this was the site that had been intended for a parliament building for such a long time during the democratic era. Marxist-Leninism, just like National-Socialism before it, excelled at organizing enormous rallies. Thus large stadiums were built to host May Day celebrations and "Spartakiad" mass spectacles of sports and dance groups, although other projects did not get off the ground, such as a huge square (designed by Kroha) near the Central Station. In the end, the political ambition to build administrative centers, research institutes, schools and university campuses was generally frustrated: "The master plan, which was worked out in the smallest detail in Soviet fashion as regards the siting of projects and the techniques to be used, often fell foul of changing realities [...] as well as personal, political and economic pressures. It became an instrument of dirigist politics, and from the moment it was approved, it was constantly being modified. So it failed to respond to the different material needs of the city and urban life."[48]

It was actually in the area of architectural heritage that the most fruitful work was carried out.[49] While the historic quarters of Prague were being revamped, the state founded the "Sírpmo" in 1954 (National Institute for the Rehabilitation of Cities and Historic Monuments), where the energies of the great architects and city planners were focused on creating a respect for history in so far as it had a specifically Czech identity. Sírpmo was in existence for forty years. First, in a number of Czech cities as well as Prague, the boundaries of the historic areas had to be defined, then the individual buildings were structurally analyzed and charted, as were their use and place in the neighborhood in which they were situated. Exceptionally rich archives were created that are still the basis of an ongoing program of conservation and rehabilitation.

"House of Fashion" store

Department store situated on Wenceslas Square,
1956. Architect: Josef Hrubý. Since demolished.

Aleksander Dubček

(1921-1992)
Leader of the Communist Party during
the "Prague Spring." He was the incarnation
of "Socialism with a human face."

Top left and right:
Invasion of Prague by the Soviet
and Warsaw Pact armies, August 21, 1968.

In 1960, Czechoslovakia officially became a "Socialist Republic." The president of the Republic, Novotný, and the man who had been the secretary of the Communist Party since 1957, had only one principle: keeping things exactly as they were. But in 1962, at the 12th Congress of the Czechoslovakian Communist Party, there was a victory for the anti-Stalinists. That very same year, urged on by Moscow, the authorities blew up Stalin's monument, and the city was rid of its cumbersome symbol. The change in the political climate gave intellectuals their chance and from 1963 onward, there was considerable ferment in cultural circles. It was the beginning of a liberalization process that led to the "Prague Spring".

Life in Prague became less dull in the decade of the 1960s. As public affairs were of no interest to anyone, people developed a consumerist mentality. This was the time when a fashion developed for little country cottages where some could escape from Prague for the weekend. Leisure activities became more varied, and thanks to the easing up of censorship and ideological control, theaters, cinemas and bookshops were able to offer a diet of greater interest and quality. Furthermore Czechoslovakia ceased to be completely isolated: in 1967, more than 300,000 people were able to visit the West. Information circulated more freely, bringing with it a radical change in lifestyle for the young (rock and roll came to Prague at the end of the 1950s).

All of these developments, the cultural ferment, the questions provoked by novels and films, the often bitter humor of plays, the changes in lifestyle, created an increasingly wide gulf between the government and the governed. The discontent of the Slovaks, stripped of their last autonomous institutions by the centralizing constitution of 1960, the crisis that the economy faced as a result of incompetent and authoritarian handling, and pressure from intellectuals were all to prove too much for Novotný.

In June 1967, the mood at the 4th Congress of the Czechoslovakian Writers' Union of was openly hostile. It went far beyond just debating the role of writers, as in 1956, but took on the regime and its policies, denouncing the "corruption" of the contemporary situation, demanding the end of censorship and addressing itself directly to political problems.

Then in 1967 the police brutally repressed a peaceful demonstration of students from the campus of Strahov University, who were protesting about their appalling living conditions, frequent cuts in electricity and hot water supplies, and others issues. This caused considerable bad feeling in the country and a wave of student unrest.

Vlasta Prachatická

Bust of Jan Palach, the twenty-year old student who burned himself to death on January 16, 1969 in protest at the invasion of August 21, 1968.
His example was followed by many others.

Finally, as a result of all this discontent and militant protest, the head of state himself was forced to resign. In January 1968, Novotný 's place as head of the Communist Party was taken by Aleksander Dubček, a man with no political program, but endowed with human qualities, such as the ability to smile (unseen since 1948). Dubček was a moderate reformer and naïvely argued for "Socialism with a human face;" on April 5, the Action Program of the Czechoslovakian Communist Party announced the intention of reforming the system from the top down. In March, Novotný was also replaced as head of state by General Svoboda (an event of symbolic interest in that "Svoboda" means "Freedom" in Czech), a hero of the Second World War, who had fought alongside the Red Army. But Dubček was soon overwhelmed by the tide of social change: free discussion everywhere, the disappearance of censorship, numerous newspaper challenges to the regime, monopoly of power by the Communist Party, and questions about the recent past. Political clubs were formed, such as the Club of the Committed Independents and Club 231, consisting of former political prisoners.

However, just like Beneš in 1945, Dubček made no allowance for Realpolitik. Neither Moscow nor the other Warsaw Pact countries could accept a change of regime in Prague. After several warnings, the "Prague Spring" was brutally snuffed out by military intervention, when on August 21, 1968, 750,000 soldiers from the Soviet Union, Poland, East Germany, Hungary and Bulgaria invaded Czechoslovakia. It was like March 1939 all over again. This time there was sporadic resis-

Street scenes in Prague
during the invasion
by the Soviet
and Warsaw Pact armies
on August 21, 1968.

tance: there were barricades, burning tanks and gunfire in the streets of Prague, and casualties.

The whole of the population supported the country's leadership, which was abducted and sequestered in the Soviert Union. There were clandestine radio broadcasts, and acts of passive resistance (Prague street names went missing), and the 14th Congress of the Communist Party also met secretly to ratify the changes and support the leadership. In spite of pressure from Moscow, a puppet government could not be formed. Dubček and his team came back to Prague and the reform process, especially in the cultural field, continued throughout 1969 if not to the beginning of 1970. The Federalization Law of October 1968 finally gave the Slovaks what they had been demanding for half a century.

However, when it was in Moscow, the Czechoslovakian leadership had signed its capitulation, accepting the permanent basing of Soviet troops in Czechoslovakia and promising to reassume control of the country. A notable measure was the re-imposing of censorship.

The population did not accept this surrender, and two students, Jan Palach in January 1969 and Jan Zajíc a month later, burned themselves to death as a public protest. Jan Palach's letter demanded the immediate lifting of all censorship and called for a massive general strike. Five hundred thousand people attended his funeral and several students went on hunger strike throughout the country.

The world ice hockey championships in Sweden in March 1969 were the scene of incidents that gave the Soviert Union and Czechoslovakian conservatives the chance to get rid of the Dubcek leadership. The Czechoslovakian team was particularly fired up and beat the Soviet team 3-2, and then went on to exploit the victory politically by protesting about the Soviet occupation of their country. The security forces and KGB used this as an opportunity to fake a provocation by stoning the Aeroflot offices and other Soviet agencies. The Soviet leadership demanded that the Prague government adopt a hard line: on April 17, 1969, Dubček was replaced by Husák at the head of the Communist Party. "Normalization" was about to set in.

On August 21, 1969, a demonstration in Wenceslas Square marking the first anniversary of the invasion was violently broken up by the police and Czechoslovakian Army. The crowd was fired upon, and there were deaths and scores of casualties.

CZECH ART
in the nineteen-sixties

The 1960s witnessed a real renaissance of Czech culture in all fields. Novels and short stories were published by Milan Kundera (*The Joke*, *Laughable Loves*), Josef Škvorecký (*The Cowards*), Ludvík Vaculík (*The Axe*, *The Guinea-pigs*) and Bohumil Hrabal (*Interminable Talkers*). Jiří Suchý and Jiří Šlitr's Semaphore Theater took up where the Liberated Theater had left off, and the Balustrade Theater performed Václav Havel's absurdist plays such as *Open Air Fête* and *The Report About You* as well as plays by Ionesco, Beckett, Jarry and Kafka. The latter had been a taboo author for a long time, first under the Nazis then under the Communists, and now came to be a symbol of cultural liberalization in the 1960s. In May 1963, a colloquium was held on Kafka's work, and resulted in his rehabilitation. The most famous Prague citizen of the twentieth century in the eyes of the outside world was finally officially accepted as part of the Prague cultural scene. The colloquium was followed by a major exhibition about the writer at the Prague Museum of National Literature.

Below (left to right):

Scene from Věra Chytilová's film *The Little Daisies*.

The Semaphore Theater with Jiří Slitr and Jiří Suchý.

Scene from Jan Němec's film *Party and Guests*.

The decade also witnessed the flowering of the Czech cinema's nouvelle vague, led by Miloš Forman (*Ace of Spades*, *The Love of a Blonde*, *The Firemen*), Věra Chytilová (*Something Different*, *Little Daisies*), Jiří Menzel (*Closely Watched Trains*, *Capricious Summer*), Evald Schorm (*Courage Each Day*, *The Verger*), Jan Němec (*The Diamonds of the Night*, *The Party and the Guests*). In 1967, Menzel's film *Closely Watched Trains*, adapted from a novel by Hrabal, won a Hollywood Oscar for best foreign film.

At the same time, there was a renewal of interest in pre-1948 Czech culture. A number of books were published about avant-garde theater of the 1920s and '30s, architecture, Poeticism, and Karel Teige's links with cinema and the world of books. In 1960 there was a retrospective on Kubišta and an exhibition on "Czech Art in the 1920s" in Brno, the same place where "The Founders of Modern Czech Art" was shown in 1957 (both exhibitions no doubt being considered too dangerous for Prague). In 1966, for the first time since 1948, an anthology of the writings of Karel Teige was published, and his collages were exhibited. Štyrský and Toyen had retrospectives in 1967, and Kupka and Šíma the following year.

Jiří John

The Table, 1972, National Gallery, Prague.

The partial liberalization of the regime after 1963 also made possible some official acknowledgement of Surrealism, for example "Symbols of Monstrosity" in 1966, the first official collective exhibition of the Prague Surrealist Group (UDS). In 1967, the Prague Group organized a major retrospective on Teige and the following year an exhibition of the Paris group's work, "The Principle of Pleasure" accompanied by a series of lectures on Surrealism and art. After the Soviet invasion, the group managed in 1969 to publish a single issue of a new periodical, *Analogon*, before it was banned.

Thanks to the new groups of artists that were set up at the end of the 1950s, things were changing in the world of art. An independent society created in 1960, the Bloc, gathered them together under its umbrella and held the "Spring 62" exhibition, which allowed them to make their mark. Bloc played an important role in overthrowing the conservative leadership of the Czechoslovakian Artists' Union. In the 1964 elections, the old leaders were voted out and Adolf Hoffmeister, a founder of Devětsil, became the head of the union.

Ever since the stirrings of 1957, Prague artists had been very active. In addition, thanks to liberalization they were well informed in the 1960s via articles and reproductions in the excellent magazine *Vtvarná Práce* and a series of exhibitions keeping them directly in touch with the work of other European creators, such as "Narrative Figuration" and "Tendencies in Contemporary Art" in 1966.

In 1960, certain young artists creating a sort of informal art called Structural Abstraction, Zdeněk Beran, Vladimír Boudník, Zbyšek Sion and Ales Veselý held unofficial exhibitions called "Confrontations I and II" in their cellar-studios. They believed in the poetry of matter in its raw state, and were so radical as to refuse to send work to the Spring 62 exhibition, to which they had been invited. They made their first showing in public in 1964, with an exhibition entitled "D," which included the work of other artists, Mikulaš Medek, Jiří Balcar and Karel Nepráš. The works exhibited were meant to be an illustration of their ideas, which were expounded in a catalogue that was denied an imprimatur. In the 1960s the first "happenings" also took place in Prague. The specialist here was Milan Knížák, the founder of the young group "Art Now" in 1963. The year after, in Novy Svět Street, they displayed giant portraits of wellknown personalities, statues and objects, and audio-visual demonstrations by Vítěk Mach. Art Now also organized a series of walkabouts and collective games that were never provocative or shocking but involved the participants. Evžen Brikcius – whom Knílák was no friend of – also organized happenings in Prague that started off as pre-arranged street incidents. His most famous happening was "Thanksgiving," performed on June 21, 1967, and culminating in the arrival of the police and arrest of the performers. Brikcius was accused of "seriously disturbing public order and offending the feelings of the workers, given that about seventy loaves of bread were used, some of them bearing messages in bad taste and having notches cut in them."

Karel Malich

Gray-Yellow Object,
circa 1962, National Gallery, Prague.

Jiři Balcar

Taking Steps Hopefully Conforming,
1968, National Gallery, Prague.

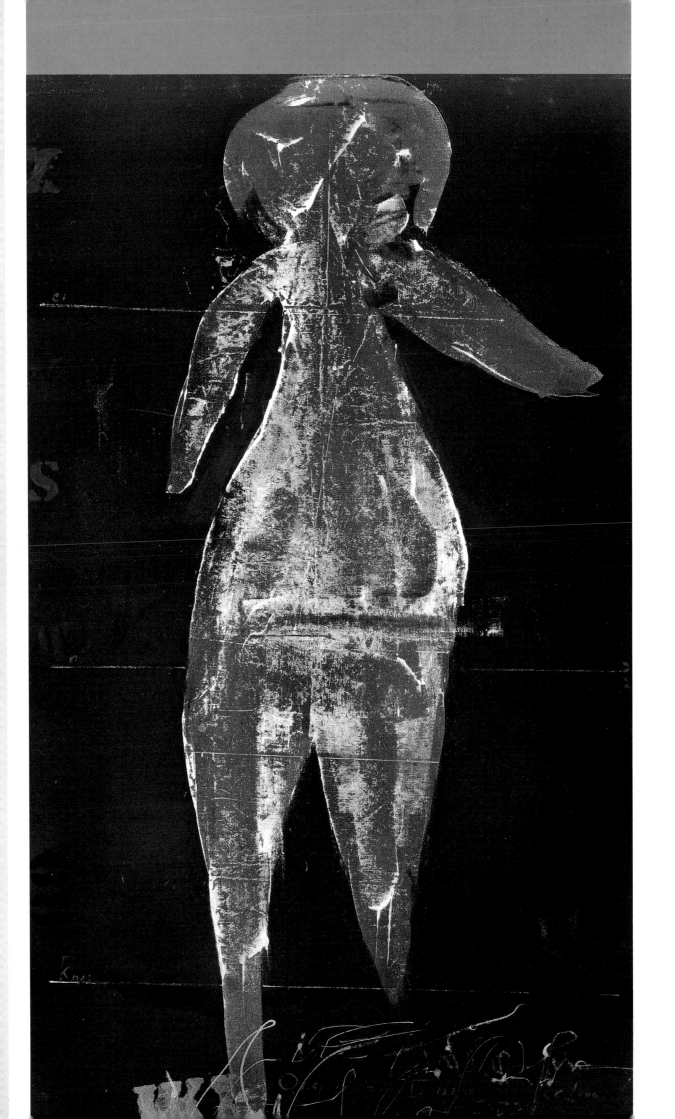

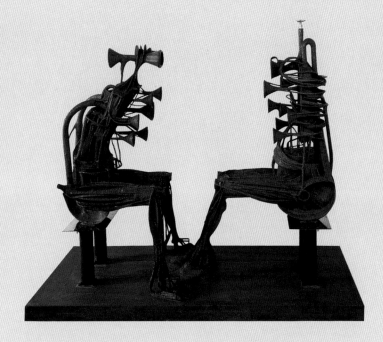

The story is symptomatic of the situation in Prague at this time and of the limits to liberalization. A few months later, the court recognized the happening as a new art form and acquitted Brikcius. In 1963-1964 the theoretician Jiří Padrta (1929-1978) was at the center of a new tendency like a sort of neo-Constructivism in keeping with the appearance of the modern world, that aspired to break with "the dominant philosophy of anguish and alienation" and with the "old metaphysical conceptions." This became apparent in the context of the "New Sensibility" exhibition in 1964, which included the work of Jiří Kolář (then making geometrical collages), Hugo Demartini, Karel Malich. Zdeněk Sykora, Václav Boštík and Alena Kučerová. Although they have in many cases gone their separate ways – Václav Boštík, for example, moved toward Lyrical Abstraction, and the visual poetry of Jiří Kolář, one of the most important Czech artists of the second half of the twentieth century, has gone way beyond Geometrical Abstraction – they had in common a rejection of "the hypertrophy of the ego," as well as of the mythology and conventional symbols of Surrealism, and a preference for an impersonal geometrical art. Zdeněk Sykora devised kinetic structures based on numerical combinations and was also the first Czech exponent of "computer painting." Malich and Demartini used very cold industrial materials such as polyester, plexiglas and chrome steel; their first exhibition aroused a lot of skepticism and general disapproval.

At the end of the 1960s, at the Picture 67 exhibition a new tendency emerged, "Radical Realism". It united two generations of artists, the one just finishing their studies and embarking upon an artistic career, such as Petra Orieškova, Peter Oriešek, Josef Vyleťal (1940-1989), and the generation born in the 1930s, having mainly been non-figurative and now peaking in the 1960s: Bedřich Dlouhý, Jaroslav Vožniak, Nadia Plíšková, Zdeněk Beran, Jiří Anderle. With all these artists the creative process generally oscillates between reality and illusion: the initial concrete object takes on more and more unreal forms. Czech "Radical Realism" is strongly influenced by the art of the fantastic and Surrealism.

Karel Nepraš

The Big Dialogue,
circa 1966-1967,
National Gallery, Prague.

Opposite page:
Stanislav Kolíbal

Half Opening,
circa 1967-1968,
National Gallery, Prague.

ARCHITECTURE AND TOWN PLANNING
REVIVAL OR *COLLAPSE?* 1958-1968

It was in 1958 in Brussels that Czech modern architecture made a recovery: the Czechoslovakian Pavilion was distinguished by its clean lines, absence of ornamentation and modern construction techniques, notably the glass elevations frankly displaying the structural features and the interior of the building. It is a design which arises from the construction admittedly, but is not devoid of poetic possibilities – very similar to what the pre-war avant-garde would have done. Quite clearly some architects were trying to escape from the Stalinist framework to something more humanist. Thus in 1961 Honzík, an ex-Devětsil member, published his novel *Remaking Paradise* about man's environment, a subject missing from political manuals. The hero was a Czechoslovakian architect, Pavel Galanda, who set off like Gauguin to seek adventure on a lonely Pacific island... The Iron Curtain could not prevent thought from wandering, or voyages from being dreamed about – the very ones that give substance to freedom. Despite these glimmerings of hope, reality was harsh and given the difficult economic situation, architectural activity was very modest: in Prague itself there were practically no more villas, houses or apartment blocks built. Public projects were put to one side, although Frágner restored the Bethlehem Chapel (now the Obce Architektu architecture gallery) and completed the rebuilding program at Charles University. Nevertheless the regime was eager to show off its modernity and technological know-how, hence the Strojimport Building, which brought the skyscraper era to Prague, and the Chemistry Institute, the facade of which was the first curtain wall in the capital. These signs of modernity were generally international as regards esthetics and strictly functional in their design and materials; they also had no regard for the existing urban scale and tended to be isolated buildings unsympathetic to the traditional street. The most ambiguous and controversial project of the decade was without a doubt the Federal Assembly, designed by Karl Prager. Admittedly the site was a prestigious one, at the top of Wenceslas Square, but it was squeezed into a corner just off the main perspective as if it were being pushed out from this grand urban area. It is also true that the commission was exceptional – a parliament building no less – but it was going to have to fit in with the equally remarkable National Museum and National Opera. In these circumstances the architect had to be ingenious. He designed an immense platform floating above the former stock exchange, and used the latter

Above left:

Czechoslovakian Pavilion

(Brussels World's Fair), 1957-1958.
František Cubr, Josef Hrubý
and Zdeněk Pokorný.
Gold Medal and two diplomas
(best architecture and best work exhibited).
The restaurant, which occupied just a part
of the pavilion, was reconstructed in Prague
in 1960 on the slopes of a hill overlooking
the Vltava. It was unfortunately damaged in
a fire in 1991, and is still waiting to be rebuilt.

Above right:

Strojimport Building

1962-1969. Zdeněk Kuna, Zdeněk Stupka
and Olivier Honke-Houfek.
Following in the footsteps of Mies
van der Rohe and Arne Jacobsen...

Sparta Stadium

1964-1968.
Architects: V. Syrovatka and C. Mandel.

as a foundation that was at least historical, if not architectural or ideological. His building is a free standing autonomous item, and unapologetically brutalist, engaging in a dialogue with its neo-Classical neighbors – a frank dialogue based on the disparity between them, rather than competition. Finally, the ground floor is spacious, open and welcoming, thanks to the bold design of the awning constituted by the floor of the parliament. The road built between these public buildings and Wenceslas Square has subsequently destroyed this last element, which was an attempt at creating urban osmosis.

Aside from these achievements, the era was a fruitful one for theoretical urban studies, particularly on the north, southwest and south suburbs of Prague. Some thought was put into the planning of the open site, block architecture with undifferentiated elevations. Not all of these projects could be achieved and the State embarked on a major program of new towns. Prague thus extended far out from the center (a surface of approximately 193 square miles for a population of 1,2 million), and thousands of housing units were built in these areas. These new residents were far from their workplace and were living in dormitory estates with few social or public facilities. Because of centralized planning, design and building were entirely in the hands of state institutions and nationalized building companies. Consequently there was a gulf between designers and consumers, and little account was taken of the needs of the latter. The quality of the building work was very dubious: dwellings had to be provided quickly, cheaply and in great number, so it was done on an industrial scale. This meant prefabricated panels with very little variation in their design, giving an overall monotonous appearance to the buildings. The dullest functional principles were the order of the day, and the whole thing was made worse by the use of poor quality materials.

Multi-purpose building (former Parliament)

1966-1972.
Architects: Karel Prager, Jiři Kadeřábek and Jiři Albrecht.
Just four piles support the base of this vast rigid
parallelepiped of girder-framed construction,
raised to the desired height by means of hydraulic jacks.

Bethlehem Chapel

1949-1953.
Rebuilt by Jaroslav Fragner.
A part of the building has since been adapted
as the Jaroslav Fragner Architecture Gallery.

Rebuilding of the Carolinum (Charles IV University),

1946-1969.
Architects: Jaroslav Fragner and Co.

PRAGUE
1970-1989
DURING THE NORMALIZATION

Normalization began with mass purges in the army, security agencies, schools and universities, cultural institutions, news media and the Communist Party. Almost 30,000 people could no longer work in their profession; in particular a quarter of the primary and secondary teaching staff lost their jobs. In 1971, the purge was completed. As was the case in 1948, there was considerable emigration, and it is estimated that between 700,000 and 800,000 people left between 1968 and 1989. Those who had lost their jobs but did not emigrate had to do something else to avoid accusations of being social parasites; so they became waiters, cigarette stall holders, boiler stokers, well-diggers, garbage collectors, window cleaners, warehousemen, street sweepers, etc. The vast majority of people soon learned to keep their mouths shut to avoid harassment, hang on to their jobs, and get their children into universities. In return the regime rewarded them with more material comfort and a developing consumer society. There were more goods in the shops, improved living standards, and the number of automobiles rose from 69,591 in 1966 to 235,000 by 1978. People devoted all their energy toward their private life. However, there was a heavy price to pay in ecological terms for this relative prosperity. Being integrated completely within COMECON (the Eastern bloc's equivalent of the Common Market) meant that Czechoslovakia had to increase its industrial production, which was twelve times what it had been in 1948. The consequences for the environment were serious, resulting in devastated forests and polluted water.

The building of the Prague metro began in 1967, and it eventually helped to improve daily life in the city, which had 1,182,294 inhabitants by 1980. It was a practical and modern system with three lines and came into operation between 1974 and 1985.

The urban landscape also underwent some changes, but they were rarely for the better. The worst aberration was the building of the north-south traffic route, a sort of urban freeway going right through the center of the city, cutting off the National Museum from Wenceslas Square, for example. Large suburban housing projects were completed, such as the South City Estate, a vast complex designed in 1972 to house 100,000 people, who were linked to the city center by metro. Cultural centers were also built in the suburbs, and they can all be lumped with the elephantine Palace of Culture (1981), the ex-Federal Parliament and the New Stage (the National Theater annex) under the term "Brutalism" coinced by certain Prague architects. The only success in town planning during the normalization period was the restoration of buildings in the conservation area around the square of the Old City, a magnificent ensemble affecting more than 2,000 historic properties.

After Czechoslovakia's ratification in August 1975 of the Helsinki Agreement, which referred to the rights of man, "dissidents" organized themselves and in January 1977, 243 people signed Charter 77. The leaders were Václav Havel, the philosopher Jan Patočka, and the man who had been foreign Minister in 1968, Jiří Hájek. The charter welcomed citizens of all persuasions, and simply requested respect for the Czechoslovakian constitution and laws that theoretically guaranteed individual freedoms. It was an opposition rallying point for the VONS, the defense committee for the wrongly imprisoned. Despite police harassment, prison sentences, and official ostracization of signatories and their families, the charter maintained a constant campaign of denouncing injustices, publishing documents for general public consumption, sending open letters and petitions to the authorities, and publicizing what was going on in Czechoslovakia abroad. By the end of 1977 almost a thousand people had signed the charter. Little by little its signatories acquired considerable moral prestige in Europe, and this was enhanced when one of them, the poet Jaroslav Seifert, was awarded the Nobel Prize for Literature in 1984.

Demonstrations between November 17, and the end of December 1989, during the "Velvet Revolution".

Street scene in Prague during the 1970s.

While all this was going on, the church experienced a revival of popularity, and religious feeling was rekindled. In 1988, 600,000 people signed a petition demanding religious freedom. All of these factors, plus the effect of political change in the Soviet Union from 1985 onward, inspired the Czechs to call upon reserves of courage and civic responsibility. Militant opposition to the regime grew much stronger after 1988. New groups came into existence, such as the Movement for Civil Liberties, the Independent Pacifist Association, the John Lennon Club, the Children of Bohemia and the Ecological Movement. A petition in June 1989, demanding the release of political prisoners, freedom of speech, association and worship, concern for the environment and an inquiry into Czechoslovakia's past, was signed by 40,000 people in six months.

Throughout 1988 and 1989, there were a number of demonstrations that were often broken up brutally by the police. On November 17, 1989, 50,000 students and secondary school pupils marched in memory of the nine students shot by the Nazis in 1939. The brutal police suppression of this march provoked the "Velvet Revolution" that eventually brought down the Communist regime. University students and theaters were among the first to call for a general strike. People invaded the streets, and there were enormous demonstrations in Wenceslas Square and on the Letná. On December 19, an opposition coordinating committee called the Civic Forum was formed, with its headquarters in the Magic Lantern Theater. The Communists knew the game was up and relinquished power. On December 29, Václav Havel was elected president of the Republic at a meeting of the Provisional Assembly chaired by a ghost from the past, Aleksander Dubček. The night of 31 December was spent by the euphoric citizens of Prague in the streets, welcoming in the New Year.

Street scenes during
the Velvet Revolution of 1989.

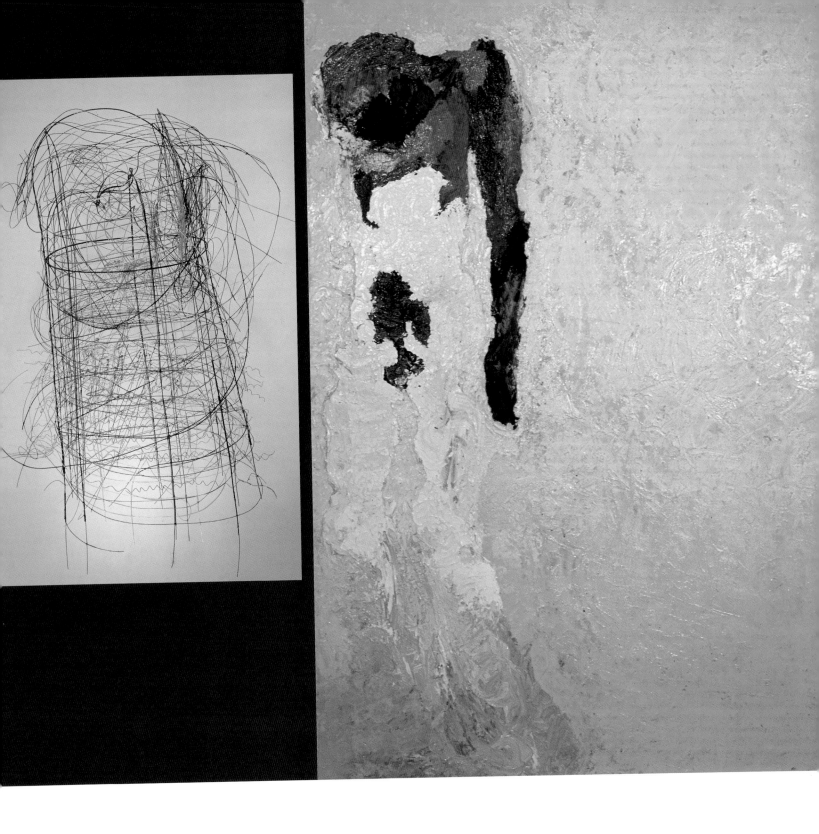

Karel Malich

Café,
circa 1985,
National Gallery, Prague.

Otakar Slavik

Untitled,
1986, private collection.

The normalization regime was suspicious of intellectuals – in September 1969, the Dubček period was referred to in the newspaper *Rudé Právo* as the "dictatorship of the Prague intellectuals" – and so Czech culture was once again put in chains. In literature, for example, the situation was catastrophic. Czech writers did their best to resist until 1970, despite coming under a lot of pressure. But books intended in 1968 for publication in 1970 were all banned, even when already printed and ready to be distributed. Finally the Czech Writers' Union was arbitrarily disbanded in October 1970. The list of banned writers, including journalists, historians, philosophers and economists, was impressive. Those writers still allowed to publish were generally distinguished by their mediocrity, with a few exceptions, such as Bohumil Hrabal. Being banned did not stop writers from publishing – this was the case with Havel notably – as their writings went round the country via *samizdat* networks or were published abroad.

A whole section of Czech culture in fact went underground. Despite constant surveillance by the security services, a certain number of people who were deprived of official existence, rebels and dissidents of various sorts managed to set up a counter-culture, a parallel society outside the official circuits. Using typewriters and carbon paper, the technology of the vital *samizdat* process, they secretly published novels, anthologies, magazines and philosophical works. The same people organized discussion groups, parallel universities, exhibitions and private performances of plays and concerts.

For the Surrealists, a clandestine existence was far from a new experience, and during the 1970s and '80s they produced a number of bulletins, generally published in Geneva. Nevertheless, certain Surrealists, such as Jan Švankmajer (born in 1934), were able to work openly and officially, in his case producing cartoon films and marionette shows that were clearly Surrealist in inspiration and sometimes very disturbing, such as *Possibility of Dialogue* in 1982. The situation in the arts was different and more complex. The Artists' Union was taken over by mediocre opportunists who seized their chance to settle accounts. They banned any group exhibitions likely to spread new ideas, and kept a tight control of permits to exhibit, whether in Prague or abroad. Yet there was a difference from the time before 1957, when ideological rectitude was what mattered; now the authorities of the union used their power to monopolize the commissioning of work for their own financial benefit. Consequently artists turned inward, just like the rest

Jiři Kolář

Homage to Christian Morgenstern,
Detail, Collage-object, undated.

of the population. There was suddenly complete chaos in artistic production, with no unity or common approach discernable any longer. The painter Jiří Sopko (born in 1942) is fairly representative of the normalization period: his work depicts a fantastical world inhabited by stupid or grotesque characters that are symbolic of a society devoid of spirituality.

The critic Jindřich Chalupecký provided a perfect analysis of the situation of Prague artists at the time in his work *New Czech Art* (written in 1985 but not published until 1994) and in articles written for Western magazines, in which he claimed that Czech art had never been more lively. The leading artists had few exhibitions between 1970 and 1985 – Kolář, Boštík (who had a big retrospective in 1987) and Adriena Šimotová. On the other hand, Kolář was one of a few who exhibited a lot abroad. And when artists "managed to find a place to hold an exhibition in, it was normally in the suburbs or in the provinces, in inappropriate and impoverished premises. The events were not advertised in the press, and there were never any reviews." But if they worked in isolation, it was because they clung to their freedom of expression at all costs, and they were not dissidents. Their stance was in no way political, and hardly any of them signed Charter 77 except Jiří Kolář, who believed himself safe enough because he was so well; he ended up emigrating to Paris, however, in 1980. Kolář in fact discouraged his fellow artists from signing in order to avoid police harassment of the artistic community in general.

Occasionally artists improvised unofficial exhibitions, like "Sculptures and Objects" in the courtyards of Malá Strana in 1981. A score of young artists exhibited their work in courtyards, on walls and in the attics of houses. The event was publicized solely by word of mouth and created a great deal of interest with the younger generation.

After 1984 a slightly more liberal attitude was taken by the regime toward the visual arts, and young artists appeared on the scene in Prague and exhibited in the suburban cultural centers. A mood of revolt could often be discerned in their work, but there was also a certain amount of naivety and immaturity. The leading names are those of the painters and sculptors of the "Hard Heads' group. Jiří David (born in 1956) started by covering his canvases with signs in the Prague hermetic tradition, then painted – and trivialized – the nation's symbols, emblems and flags. Stanislas Diviš (born in 1953) painted pictures reminiscent of diagrams derived from scientific photographs; Michal Gabriel (born in 1960) sculpted hybrid birdman creatures; the draftsman and sculptor František Skála (born in 1956) made poetic objects that defy classification, creating a mysterious universe, primitive and fantastic at the same time. In 1987, the "Hard Heads" were allowed to exhibit for the first time in Prague, and even met with a measure of approval in the official press.

At the end of 1987, an interesting exhibition entitled "The Grotesque in Twentieth Century Czech Art" was held in the Prague Town Hall. It featured the "soft" sculptures and environments of Kurt Gebauer (born in 1941), metallic anthropoid sculpture by Karel Nepraš (a member of the onetime Šmidrové group), Jiří Sopko's characters without depth, and the comic monsters with occasionally explicit titles like "Frogman" or "Crucified Man with Helmet" made by Ladislav Novák (born in 1925), an artist on the Surrealist fringe and drawn to visual poetry, like Jiří Kolář.

The series entitled "Contemporary Czech Art," published by Odeon at the end of the 1970s and beginning of the '80s, was of some significance. Although some of the work was very poor, it did include important contemporary authors like Jiří John, Adriena Šimotová, Jiří Anderle, Naděžda Plíšková, Vladimír Preclík, Daisy Mrázková, Petr Hampl, Zdeněk Sýkorá, Jiří Sopko, Jiří Sozanský. The last named, an engraver, painter, sculptor, creator of installations and environments and director of "filmed actions," is one of the most disturbing contemporary Prague artists from the aesthetic point of view.

Curiously, there were loopholes in the system. Some organizations, such as suburban arts centers and provincial museums, were less strictly supervised than others. Even in Prague itself the little theater in Neruda Street and the "Jazz Section" (Prague's experimental jazz and rock center that

Jiři Načeradský
Double portrait,
circa 1980,
National Gallery, Prague.

was finally closed by the police in September 1977), directed by one of the figureheads of underground culture, the music critic Karel Srp, put on interesting events and published brochures and catalogues. Exhibitions of good quality were put on in the theater in Neruda Street between 1975 and 1979, covering a wide range of contemporary Czech art: painting, sculpture, drawing, engraving, photography, collage, fabric wall-hangings and ceramics. There was never a trace of Socialist Realist inspiration, and the variety and quality of the work exhibited shows how slender was the ideological divide between permitted and forbidden art.

During the normalization period, a real underground culture developed, in which poets such as Egon Bondy and a number of musicians and singers flourished on the margins of official society. After 1970, the authorities clamped down on rock groups, particularly those singing in English. The only alternative for those unwilling to conform was to go underground and live in a parallel universe; this is what Plastic People of the Universe did, the most famous group of the era, who performed in barns for private parties in villages around Prague. All the leaders of this counter-culture were of working class origin, and the authorities generally attacked them for their "obscenity." Some of their songs actually conveyed a deep hatred of the regime, which the latter naturally felt threatened by, so the police felt empowered to harass them with impunity, as they were outside traditional intellectual circles and thus relatively defenseless. In 1976 Plastic People of the Universe was arrested, which had an impact on Prague's dissident intellectuals, however, and was one of the events leading up to the birth of Charter 77, which many members of the underground in fact joined.

The underground universe was also the place where the man who is now the bestknown Czech photographer in the world began creating; this is Jan Saudek (born in 1935), who had been a worker in a printing press since 1950. He began by photographing invented scenes of a baroque nature that were both erotic and grotesque, depicting usually nude figures in a timeless universe. His studio was his cellar, and he used its shell-covered walls for a background and just a few accessories to create a universe that would appear to be the exact opposite of the Art Nouveau-inspired Romantic clichés of Drtikol.

Zdeněk Sýkora
Line n°50,
circa 1985,
National Gallery, Prague.

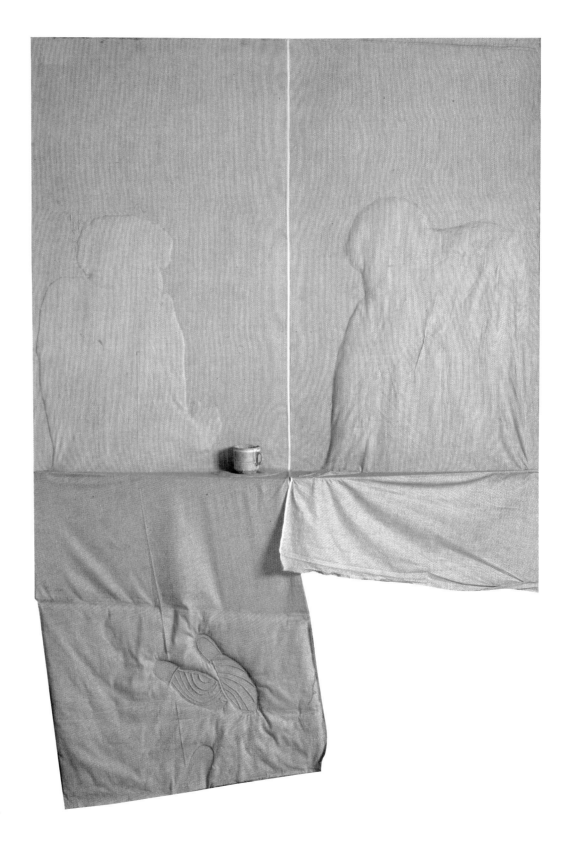

Adriena Šimotová

Close Distancing,
1976-1977,
National Gallery, Prague.

ARCHITECTURE AND TOWN PLANNING

1968-1989

EXCESS or NORMALIZATION?

To tackle the accommodation crisis, the state extended its program of satellite towns, as was the policy everywhere in Europe. Once again it was a question of mass-produced cheap dwellings in large estates lacking facilities and situated far from the historic center. In other words, as we have already stated, dormitory towns. On the outskirts of Prague in 1972, the "South City" project was launched, with the intention of accommodating 100,000 people no less. To create a human feeling, some of the features of garden cities were borrowed, such as landscaping and making the best use of undulating terrain. On the other hand provision of facilities was poor, other than cultural centers. The estate was served by the metro so that it was not geographically isolated or cut off from the capital. The metropolitan area was now vast, and providing efficient services became a planning priority. Public transport naturally had an important part to play, especially a bus and tram network, being easy to install. A far bigger operation was the building of the Prague metro, which was more difficult technically and more expensive. Work on it started in 1967 and went on until the three lines were opened between 1974 and 1985. Finally a program of road building was an inevitable part of development, and this was to have a big impact on the layout and cityscape of Prague. However it came later than public transport, first because Skoda automobiles were expensive and there was a long waiting list for them, and then it took a long time to devise a scheme that met with general approval. The problem was to remove congestion from the historic center and make the city's traffic flow efficient. Although an outer ringroad was much debated, an Americanstyle north-south through road was the solution adopted. This was the Magistralá, a six-lane urban freeway built between 1975 and 1978. Scant respect in its planning was paid to the city center, as it cuts off the Wilson Railway Station from the city and the National Museum and the Parliament building from Wenceslas Square. In both cases these were buildings whose raison d'être required them to be part of the fabric of the city and with a quick and easy access; and they were also essential to the physical and visual coherence of Prague. The Magistralá destroys this osmosis by cutting these public buildings off from their substratum and marginalizing them, so that they are nothing more than urban side-shows.

There was also a certain amount of architectural activity stemming from public projects to fill gaps in the provision of facilities and head offices. Most were built around the edges of the historic center (without much thought about the context), and occasionally in the city center in the case of the most prestigious. The Socialist regime gave its blessing to consumerism and authorized the building of large stores and shopping centers, two examples of which are the Kotva department store, with its overlapping hexahedral design and unrelated elevations on a very restricted site, so typical of the 1960s, and the K-Mart store (as it now is) with more restrained lines harmonizing with the scale and alignment of its neighbors. Prague also had to tackle a shortfall in hotel provision. The Intercontinental and the Hilton, built at an interval of twenty years, were both attempts to import the latest ideas of luxury and comfort, notably in materials and color schemes, at the risk of quickly going out of date. The Praha, which was more specifically designed for Czech or foreign Communist dignitaries, was allocated a hillside setting for its curved design. Although they gave the hotel a rather defensive appearance from the outside, its designers were not stinting in the scale of construction and luxurious design and facilities: use of traditional noble materials (marble, etc), huge swimming pool and vast panorama. The state was also keen to make an impression with more prosaic (but very visible) projects, such as Hubácek's water tower and the radio and television

Intercontinental Hotel

interior,
1968-1974.
Architects: Karel Filsák, Karel Bubeniček and Jaroslav Švec.

K-Mart department store (formerly Maj store)

1970-1975.
Architects: Miroslav Masák, John Eisler and Martin Rajniš.

Věra Chytilova's Villa

1970-1975.
Architect: Emil Přikryl.

Above:

Retirement home

1973-1978.
Architects: Jan Linek
and Vlado Milunič.

Right:

Shopping center

1977-1990.
Architects: Ladislav Lábus
and Alena Šrámková.

Intercontinental Hotel

1968-1974
Architects: Karel Filsák,
Karel Bubeníček and Jaroslav Švec.

Following page:

Office blocks

Wenceslas Square, 1975-1982.
Architects: Alena and Jan Šramek
(left, an 18thcentury building, right,
the Koruna Building (1911-1914).

transmitter, the first of which demonstrated expertise in the use of molded glass and aluminum, and the second in the mastery of heights (and of the media). Finally, there is the saga of the National Theater. It will be remembered that it was destroyed by fire a few days before it was due to open, then completely rebuilt out of the proceeds of a national subscription fund (1868-1883). The centenary of its opening was a chance for the regime to commemorate Czech history. The planned enlargement of the theater also led to the symbolic exaggeration of the word "national". A first phase extension between 1977 and 1981 provided offices for administrators and rehearsal rooms. The second expansion, to the north, included a foyer and a new stage (Nova Scéna). This time the architect took a radical decision: the old and new buildings are separate from each other, and their style and scale are antagonistic. The Nova Scéna is first of all an urban development that leaves the ground floor free and opens up the site for pedestrians to walk through. But then it is a massive piece of uncompromising and forthright architecture with no historical or neo-Classical stylistic context, embedded in a spectacular box of brick and glass. It is a work that has an exterior impact, since the lights from the performance filter through the walls and sunlight is diffracted by the textured surface of the glass, as well as being distinctive on the inside, as the auditorium is housed in this cocoon and bathed in a uniform, velvety atmosphere. The urge to demonstrate the modernity of Prague as well as of the country, to compete with the West in doing so, also meant that administrative buildings had to be imposing. So they were often large isolated masses, impressive in their scale and lines but unrelated to their urban surroundings. It needs to be said that these prestige buildings put a lot of pressure on budgets, and their technical effectiveness was heavily reliant on Western builders and suppliers. Good examples are the Kovo Building and the CKD Company Building. The latter was one of the first to tend toward postmodernism, in this case the eclectic geometrical tendency, using primary shapes from the sharp edge to the curve, and trying to introduce a few breaks in the surface of an elevation that is otherwise strikingly lacking in thickness. There were other postmodernist ventures, such as the building used for storing materials – as it happens, banned literature. A symbolically appropriate use for such a piece of architecture.

Motokov Building

1975-1977.
Architects: Zdeněk Kuna, Olivier Honke-Houfek,
Zdeněk Stupka, Milan Valenta and Jaroslav Zdražil.

Recycling plant

1977-1984.
Architect: Tomáš Brix.

"Kovo" Office Building

1974-1977.
Architects: Z. Edel, J. Matyaš, C. Štefek, and P. Štech.

Building work also went on in the historic center of the city, with mixed results. What of the heritage dimension? After the 1968 normalization, the retirement of the Frágner generation of architects and the considerable decline in Sírpmo 's activities, the conservation policy was extended to take in the "new" city, particularly the late nineteenth century quarters. Restoration work was carried out, for example, on the Saint George Convent, the Lobkowicz Palace and the renaissance ceilings of the Martinic Palace. The normalization period must also be given credit for restoring the historic area around the Old Town Square, which includes more than 2,000 old houses. But in Prague generally the conservation measures adopted are ineffective. If Lukeš[50] is to be believed, many districts laid out at the end of the nineteenth and beginning of the twentieth centuries were badly neglected in the 1970s, for example Žižkov, Vysočany, Smíchov, Bíevnov and Střeřovice. The state actually preferred to demolish an old building rather than maintain it, and replace it by a building using the modern prefabrication methods of the new mass estates (and with the same monotonous results). There was also some destruction in the castle, particularly of Plecnik's work: "Both inside and out, most of his work was destroyed between 1970 and 1989, and it is practically impossible to restore it to its original condition[51]". Yet the 1980s were marked by fresh interest in the old quarters, and there was talk of a (cautious) modernization of the habitat, and some rehabilitation of architectural heritage carried out.[52] In the final reckoning, conservation and restoration were frequently thwarted during the period of Communist rule because of numerous problems.[53] On the one hand, the State did not possess the necessary resources to finance work on nationalized buildings, which at least meant that a halt was put to demolition even if there was no money to maintain the heritage. On the other, existing regulations were insufficient to prevent local councils from doing whatever they wanted, i.e., demolish. It is calculated that 10 percent of listed buildings have disappeared in this way, and many others are in a dilapidated state.

Shopping center

1977-1990.
Ladislav Lábus and Alena Šrámková.

National Theater – "Nova Scena"

Above: the old facade,
1881-1883.
Architects: Josef Zitek and Josef Schulz.

Above left: the new building,
1980-1983.
Architect: Karel Prager
(for the Prague Building Institute).

A ceiling of 4,306 glass bricks, each measuring
32 by 24 by 16 inches and weighing 88 pounds.

Water tower

1974-1975.
Architects: Karel Hubáček and Zdeněk Patrman.

In 1990, after a terrible hiatus of fifty years, Prague seemed to be reborn. The city got rid of the symbols of the old regime. Little by little a certain number of streets were renamed to reestablish the link with national traditions (Masaryk was given back his station and his quayside, the Czechoslovakian Legions their bridge) or to commemorate the sacrifice of victims of Communism (Jan Palach, and Milada Horáková, who was hanged in 1950). In June 1990, the first free elections took place since 1946.

The fall of the Communist regime brought the end of cohabitation between Czechs and Slovaks. Their divorce was finalized on January 1, 1993. Henceforth Prague was the capital of the Czech Republic, with Václav Havel as its first president.

As borders were opened up and economic liberalism triumphed, Prague changed a lot. The city where time seemed to stand still finally took its place in the modern era. Private shops and smart bars replaced the austere state establishments, department stores were well stocked, and the formerly drab trams were covered in advertisements. The city was one of the top tourist destinations in Europe, and the extraordinary tourist boom brought with it a growth in tertiary sectors and services. The aesthetic gain for the city was considerable. Many facades were cleaned up and restored, and certain old quarters that had been abandoned, or disfigured by scaffolding, came back to life.

Despite problems stemming from the change to a market economy, the country's economy is reliable. It attracts foreign capital, and the unemployment rate is one of the lowest in Central Europe. Prague is also reassuming its place in Europe, and is now the home of the permanent secretariat of the CSCE (Conference on Security and Cooperation in Europe). The Czech Republic is now a member of NATO, and is also one of the countries whose application to become a member of the European Union has been officially accepted. Entry into the union is expected in a few years.

Vaclav Hável

At the time of his election, with the emblem of the Czech Republic behind him, the lion with two tails.

The immense statue of Klement Gottwald, disgraced first president of the Communist era, being demolished in Prague in November 1989.

The Czech foreign minister, Jiří Diensbien and his Austrian counterpart, Alios Mock, cutting the barbed wire on the Austro-Czech border near Kleinhaugsdorf.

Removing Soviet era emblems, November 1989.

Jiří Černý

The Pink Tank,
A monument built in 1945 in homage
to the Red Army after the liberation of Prague,
repainted clandestinely by the artist on
two occasions in 1991.

since 1990

In the cultural field, the return to democracy meant the disappearance of the official structures of the old regime; the symbols of Communism and the more ostentatious products of Socialist Realism went to the junkyard. And while certain "artists" and "writers" of the normalization era were permanently laid off, the boundary between "approved" and "underground" artists vanished. Market forces came into the world of Czech art, with sometimes chaotic results. The ecstatic thrill of freedom following the Velvet Revolution together with a dedication to earning money any way possible was not necessarily an ideal formula for a flourishing culture. Thus while a great number of banned books were published, small publishing companies came into existence to create leisure reading of no great merit. There was a risk that the sudden confrontation with market values might have unfortunate consequences: the traditional seriousness, profundity and spirituality of Czech art might suffer by comparison with what was modish, superficial and commercially profitable.

And yet art in Prague did retain a degree of independence, partly thanks to a private organization, the Soros Center for Contemporary Arts, which was set up in 1992 and gave remarkable support to artistic creativity. It partly took over a role that the state could no longer handle, helping artists by giving them access to new technology, awarding them bursaries and organizing exhibitions. Thus the "Orbis Fictus" exhibition in 1994-1995 exhibited work derived from information technology. There was nothing artificial about this in Prague; rather it harked back to an old tradition of a hazy boundary between the real and the unreal – the realm of the virtual – in a city where the writer Karel Čapek invented the term "robot" and the artist Zdeněk Pešánek experimented with kinetic sculpture between the wars.

Whereas Jiří Sopko had acquired the status of a "classic" Prague artist of the 1990s, the dominant trends in Czech art today are represented mainly by those who receive the Jindřich Chalupecký Prize, created in 1990 on the initiative of Václav Havel, the painter Theodor Pištěk (one of the rare Czech exponents of Hyperrealism) and Jiří Kolář. Among the prize-winners, apart from two members of the "Hard Heads" group, František Skála (1991) and Michal Gabriel (1994), and Vladimír Kokolia (1990), all three of whom were born in the 1950s, there are mostly younger artists of the generation of the '60s: Michal Nesázal (1992), Martin Mainer (1993), Kateřina Vincourová (1996) and the sculptor Jiří Přihoda (1997). Kokolia is a painter, draftsman and engraver who creates a strange universe full of disturbing symbols – in 1990, he painted a series of canvases full of mice; Nesázal varies between a "distanced" figurative style that looks almost virtual and decorative abstraction; Vincourová dreams up installations, in which it is normally possible to enter, re-creating artificial magic worlds inspired by events in her life or by her dreams (her favorite material is rubber); Mainer focuses a lot on the collective culture of the nation, and makes no secret of his respect for both Kupka and Váchal; Přihoda, a pupil of Stanislav Kolíbal, is attracted to the theme of man's impact on nature, and uses elementary shapes to play with the ambiguity of the material world.

Generally speaking, Czech artists are marked personally by having been semi-clandestine. Thus they remain essentially individualistic, seldom identifying with the real world, and drawing on intimate experience for their art. However, the "Trial Run" exhibition in 1995, a showplace for the very youngest generation, contained a large body of work in which real social concerns were apparent. One of the exhibitors was Jiří Černický, who went on to win the Jindřich Chalupecký Prize in 1998. The Soros Center's role in encouraging a degree of "socialization" of art is far from negligible. For example, the "Public Art" project that it supported in 1997-1998 was an interesting attempt at bringing modern art to the city. A great number of projects were submitted with the intention of making an impact on certain open spaces in the city. Some were fairly conventional, such as painting frescos on the facades of buildings, others were more "off the wall," such as Michal Sedlák's idea for

Jiří Černický

Crystal Heroin,
sculpture, 1996.

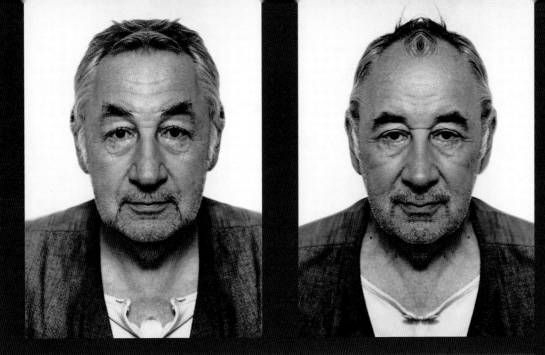

Jiří David

Hidden Image, circa 1995,
morphed portrait of the French actor, Philippe Noiret.

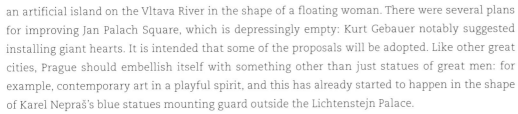

an artificial island on the Vltava River in the shape of a floating woman. There were several plans for improving Jan Palach Square, which is depressingly empty: Kurt Gebauer notably suggested installing giant hearts. It is intended that some of the proposals will be adopted. Like other great cities, Prague should embellish itself with something other than just statues of great men: for example, contemporary art in a playful spirit, and this has already started to happen in the shape of Karel Nepraš's blue statues mounting guard outside the Lichtenstejn Palace.

One of the most positive aspects of Czech art in the last decade is without a doubt the effort that has been made to reestablish continuity with the past. At the beginning of 1990, the Prague House of Photography was opened; where the work of Drtikol, Funke, Rössler, Reichmann, Hak and Zykmund has since been exhibited here. In the same year, an old artistic organization dating back to 1863 was re-founded, the l'Umělecká Beseda. Then a decision taken by the Communist regime in 1978 was implemented; this was to complete the conversion of the Exhibition Center to house the Museum of Modern Art. It opened in December 1995, but not without controversy as far as the selection of modern Czech was concerned: for example, the Šmidrové of the 1960s are almost absent. Finally, the Museum of Czech Cubism, located in the House of the Black Madonna, opened its doors in 1994.

While all this was going on, big exhibitions were held that also harked back to Prague's past. One of them was "Czech Art Deco" (1993), featuring a movement that the Communist regime had disapproved of because it was typical of the bourgeois republic of the interwar years. Another, in 1994, was devoted to the work of Karel Teige (1900-1951) and in 1996 there was a superb retrospective of Czech Surrealism, the first in Prague since 1946. And nearly ten years after it was written, Jindřich Chalupecký's fundamental work *New Czech Art* was at last published.

Indeed, what the people of Prague need more than novelty is a return to the past, to reclaim whole sections of their culture hidden by the Communist regime. They need to reconstruct their fragmented knowledge of their traditions. Thus there is a passionate interest in Masaryk, and books are written about the Czech Legions and the country's military involvement in both world wars. In the artistic field, too, there is a need to know more, particularly about the artists who had to exhibit clandestinely after 1970. In this spirit, there has been a series of exhibitions about the great names of the 1960s, like Eva Kmentová (who died in 1980), Adriena Šimotová, Věra Janoušková, Daisy Mrázková ou Vladimír Janoušek. Likewise the Czech Surrealists have held a number of collective exhibitions and revived their magazine *Analogon* after a break of twenty-one years.

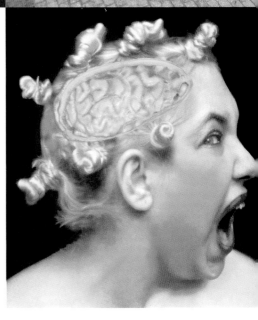

Veronika Bromová

Scenes,
digital photography,
1996, private collection.

František Skala

Sorcerer,
circa 1995,
National Gallery, Prague.

The important "Roots" exhibition in 1997 also emphasized the continuity of art in Prague by including artists of the '60s (born in the '20s), like Václav Boštík, Karel Malich and Adriena Šimotová alongside the generation of the '80s (born in the '50s), like Ivan Kafka, creator of minimalist installations, Vladimír Kokolia and Martin Mainer.

Prague now has an excellent fortnightly art magazine called *Atelier*, and artists as well as the general public can keep abreast of developments at home and abroad. Czech culture is slowly resuming its place in the world. There are more and more foreign exhibitions, even if they are mainly about Czech art of the pre-1945 era. The renewal of cultural life is taking place too in other media: in 1997 Jan Svěrák's film *Kolya* received the Oscar for Best Foreign Film, and this director is regarded by many critics as the rising star of the Czech cinema industry.

Jiří Černický

Masks,
installation, 1996,
private collection.

Forest Carpet for a Random
Mushroom Picker,
designed 1989,
created October 1991, October
1993, October 1995, October 1996.
Artist's collection.

Adriana Šimotová

Fear,
1984, private collection.

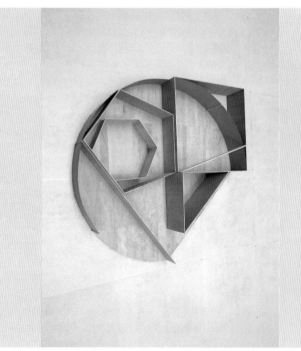

Stanislas Kolíbal

Construction,
circa 1990, National Gallery, Prague.

Michal Gabriel

Scribe,
National Gallery, Prague.

Petr Nikl

Expelled from Paradise,
no date,
National Gallery, Prague.

Kateřina Vincourová

Sunday,
1987,
National Gallery, Prague.

A CITY IS AN ENSEMBLE THAT MUST STAY INDEFINITELY
AND STRUCTURALLY NOT SATURABLE, OPEN ON ITS OWN
TRANSFORMATION, ON ENLARGEMENTS THAT AFFECT OR DISPLACE
THE MEMORY OF ITS HERITAGE AS LITTLE AS POSSIBLE. A CITY MUST STAY
OPEN ABOUT THE FACT THAT IT DOES NOT YET KNOW WHAT IT WILL
BECOME: RESPECT FOR THIS NOT-KNOWING MUST HAVE A THEMATIC
PLACE IN SCIENCE AND IN THE COMPETENCE OF ARCHITECTS
AND TOWN PLANNERS
JACQUES DERRIDA [54]

The IPS Building

(the national electricity company),
1998.
Architects: Zdeněk Jiran,
Michal Kohout, Lukáš Holub
and Lubor Sladký.

In addition to having social and political consequences, the Velvet Revolution transformed the legislative and economic context of the country. Communes (including Prague) became responsible for their own management, real estate was gradually handed back to individuals and companies, and foreign investors were soon knocking at the door of this new national market. These factors had a brutal impact on the commissioning of new work and the way it was financed by opening up patronage to private clients and changing the status of architects. Prague took the decision to exploit its exceptional heritage to the maximum, which got it on to UNESCO's World Heritage list in 1992, and then faced up to mass tourism. Experience shows that this can have unfortunate consequences: ruining the fabric of local shopping areas, emptying historic centers of their population and destroying the soul of certain old quarters and their local culture by internationalizing and trivializing them. Fortunately the city of Prague quickly anticipated these dangers, and has sought to reconcile economic development and protection of her heritage, in particular by studying the experience of other European countries. In immediate concrete terms, the tourist windfall has brought about improvements in the transport networks, such as the inner and outer ring-roads, and the rehabilitation of certain major tourist sights and monuments. But there are still failings in the mechanism for protecting the heritage, some of them in the area of legislation (the conservation authorities have access only to limited regulations and laws, and inadequate staff to enforce them), others of a financial nature (the city has limited funds and state subsidies are symbolic). Tourism is also of interest to those who have retaken possession of their old property. Suddenly they are faced with the cost of renovation and maintenance, and many have adopted the solution of selling or renting out apartments or converting the ground floor into a shop or business. The impact on the city is naturally considerable, as there are thousands of such buildings. At ground floor level their appearance has been completely changed, and although the results so far vary from district to district, the general impression is that the city is not too adversely affected.

since 1990

The ABC Office Block

1992-1994.
Martin Kotík,
Václav Králíček
and Vladimír Krátký.

An incidental effect is that the various building trades involved have expanded to cope with all the renovations, alterations to interiors, fitting out of apartments, shops, cafés, restaurants, etc. The freeing up of the market has undeniably been advantageous for the city, complete districts and individual blocks of buildings. The new owners make a careful choice of architect to enhance their property. A good example of a successful rehabilitation is one done on a block of apartments for rent by the architect Lábus. It was essentially a matter of restoring the ground floor frontages and making alterations to the layout of several apartments. The architect opted for creating an open plan habitat, allowing large diagonal perspectives and maximum light penetration in general and from one room to another. Corridors are minimized, as unnecessary walls and partitions have been taken out; sliding partitions and screens with transparent panels allow for great flexibility in the use and appearance of rooms. While the design is characteristic of this architect, there is another aspect of this commission that applies to a number of similar ones in Prague, and that is the high standard of the fittings used, matched by a comparable level of craftsmanship, as can be seen in the attention to minute detail and careful assembly, and in the quality of the materials.

The same is also undoubtedly true of certain prestige projects, like the one in Prague Castle, where Pleskot has used the opportunity to demonstrate his architectural convictions. Although the space involved presented no problem and the materials were conventional, he managed to make this restaurant look like an architect's drawing, remarkable for its geometrical rigor (enhanced by refined patterning) and meticulous craftsmanship. This combination is also found in numerous galleries, where the strength and inventiveness of the design are perhaps in the process of constituting a Prague "school". This conceptual elegance conveys a visceral loathing for the mass-produced dwellings in the dormitory suburbs as well as a healthy reaction against the market economy.

This professional code of values is also to be found in the new relationship between the architect and the commissioning body, as is remarkably demonstrated by the Koucky firm. The client gains access to this via an almost ritual journey. After leaving the street, he goes round the side of a building, and suddenly finds that the practice is literally exposed before his eyes – every aspect of its activities can be seen through a vast glass wall. The detail is not insignificant when we remember that this architect is both a theoretician and the winner of several prizes, and it actually says a lot about a profession that has to define its role and its constitution in a country that has rediscovered liberal economics.

Another new factor, as we have said, is the appearance on the scene of foreign investors who buy building plots (often sold by the municipality). The projects are generally offices or hotels, frequently designed by a foreign architect in collaboration with a Czech partner. This was the case with the Myslbeck and ABC buildings, and also the building designed by the Californian Frank O'Gehry, dumped there awaiting a future use. The architect has linked up two irregular cylinders, one a swaying, supple Spanish dancer in skirts of glass and steel stiffeners, the other a jaunty matador in a rendered waistcoat and countless medals: the building was nicknamed "Ginger and Fred." Even more surprising are the undulating lines that follow the isometric contours of the site, and the projecting windows with jutting frames that compensate for the slenderness of the facade. Those more kindly disposed could see here an interpretation of baroque or Cubist extravaganza so dear to Prague. Another architect in vogue is Jean Nouvel, who is responsible for no fewer than three projects of substance. One is an urban study for the whole of the Smíchov district; the other two (the Anděl and ING projects) are developments on the scale of a complete block. They are both now going up, and the drawings point to a basic concern for the historic and urban context, enlivened by good measures of technical inventiveness, poetic narration and formal ease.

The National Dutch Insurance Company Building

1992-1996.
Frank O. Gehry and Associates, with Vlado Milunič.
Built on an Anglo-American bombsite on the edge
of the river.

Offices

Interior and exterior, 1993-1994.
Architect: ADNS agency.

since 1990

Aréàl Hvezda Petřiny

1998. Architect: Vlado Milunic.

Czech architects are not to be outdone and have designed buildings of significance. The ADNS partnership is capable of combining the best of Czech and western architecture. The proof of this was the Czechoslovakian pavilion for the World's Fair in Seville (which was itself an architectural homage to Krejcar's pavilion for the Paris World's Fair of 1937). The partnership is also responsible for an office block in Prague of a well-handled functional design enhanced by verdigris granite elevations and gray-blue terrazzo entrance flooring. A number of projects have only just been completed, and the exemplary IPS Building may be singled out for mention: in a part of the city where the urban fabric is about to give way to fields, the architects have erected an orthogonal building completely occupying the block; the adjacent streets are clearly demarcated, but the main point is that a central pedestrian walkway is created which, by skillful use of changes in level and materials, effects a gentle transition from public to private areas. It is also an interesting mixed use development: on the one hand offices with "professional" facades; on the other, apartments that benefit from the sun, the humanity of a brick building no more than four stories high, and the fantasy of a tower.

The "selected items" in this work represent only a fraction of the architectural achievement to be found in the Czech Republic. This is especially the case in the last decade, when the architects mentioned have also been busy outside Prague. The reader who wishes to be better informed about them, as well as about others too numerous to mention, could fruitfully consult Czech periodicals such as *Zlatý řez* (Golden Number) or the annual publications that introduce the com-

petitors for the national prizes (Grand Prix - Obce architektá, with summaries in English and rich iconography). These publications are the work of architects and historians who are in some measure reviving the critical consciousness of the avant-garde between the world wars – an excellent development. Certain architects who are once again willing to teach and pass on knowledge also share this intellectual attitude. In exemplary fashion, Emil Přikryl, whose work revitalized architecture in the 1980s, has ceased to practice; he has become a professor at the Academy of Fine Arts, in the tradition of his eminent predecessor Jan Kotěra.

The Velvet Revolution was also a stone revolution: for some time Prague was a teeming building site with a forest of props and shuttering, which without any doubt reunited architects and clients with the resourceful past of their city. Although residents are moving out of the historic nucleus of the city, and the European economic crisis is beginning to bite, with the result that building projects are clearly slowing down, optimism nevertheless prevails. The architects of the new generation are talented enough to make the best of any situation, and possessed of sufficient elegance to design architecture in a humanist tradition.

Entrance to the Lví Dvůr restaurant

1995. Josef Pleskot, Radek Lampa, Jana Vodičkova and Peter Lacko.

Courtyard of the Lví Dvůr restaurant

1995. Josef Pleskot, Radek Lampa,
Jana Vodičkova and Peter Lacko.

Myslbek Complex

1993-1996. Architects: Claude Parent,
with Zdeněk Hölzel and Jan Kerel.

**Myslbek Complex
(internal courtyard and facade)**

1993-1996. Claude Parent,
with Zdeněk Hölzel and Jan Kerel.
The diagonal lattice slides on rails,
opening in the day and closing at night,
a reminder of the medieval precinct
which once occupied part of the plot.

since 1990

Refurbished apartment block

1998, Ladislav Lábus.

Opposite page:

Redesign of a 19th century building as offices and flats

1993-1995. Architect: DA Studio
(Martin Rajniš, Stanislas Fiala, Tomaš Prouza,
Jaroslav Zina).

Internal layout of an apartment

1996. Architects: Ivan Kroupa and Tomaš Novotný.

The Roman Koucký Partnership offices

1998. Architect: Roman Koucký.

since 1990

The Andel Complex

Completed in 2000,
Architect: Jean Nouvel.

NOTES

1 Mainly via World's Fairs, which were extremely successful and served as a showcase
for booming new materials, techniques and projects. They were a factor in the progressive erosion of existing dogma in aesthetics.

2 The Mánes group (founded in 1887 and including architects) called for an art that was both Czech and modern. In 1894 the artists signed the Manifesto of Czech Modernity, and a year later Prague hosted an Ethnographic Exhibition in which the country's popular art was presented to the public for the first time. A gulf opened up between Prague and "official" art centered on Vienna. The philosopher Masaryk was also keenly interested in the question of Czech identity (česká otázka – The Czech Question, 1895), as was F. X. Šalda (the founder of modern Czech criticism), for whom "every strong and healthy nation that cares about its education must have its own national art and science: they cannot be those of another country" (Kritické projevy – Critical Discourses, 1910-1911).

3 the end of the 19th century architects launched the "Czech Renaissance", an eclectic style with a neo-Classical bias. Apart from the buildings designed by Antonin Wiehl and Jan Koula, the best known are the National Theater (Josef Schulz and Josef Zítek, 1868-1883; considered to be "an event of the first order" by Janák), the Rudolphinum (Schulz and Zítek, 1874-1885), the monumental National Museum at the top end of Wenceslas Square (Schulz, 1885-1890), and the Museum of Decorative Arts (Schulz, 1897-1901). The Czechs wanted to show what they were capable of, and also rouse the national conscience allegorically.

4 Five different terms exist for this: Art Nouveau, Jugendstil, liberty, modern style, Secession (in Central Europe). Following on from the Arts and Crafts movement, Art Nouveau developed in Belgium (Victor Horta and Paul Hankar – the Hôtel Tassel, Brussels, 1893), spread to Paris (Hector Guimard, Castel Béranger; Galerie Bing, 1895), then Vienna (Otto Wagner, Joseph Maria Olbrich), Prague and Munich (Auguste Endell, Richard Riemerschmid). It then became more widely European during the first decade of the 20th century: Barcelona (Antoni Gaudí), Darmstadt, Glasgow (Charles Rennie Mackintosh), Helsinki, Nancy (Emile André), Turin and Weimar (Henry Van de Velde). The style disintegrated and fell out of fashion just before the First World War.

5 At this time, Europe "borrowed from industry the strength and the lightness of its castings," in the words of Joris-Karl Huysmans (L'Art moderne – Modern Art, 1883). The famous example was Hector Guimard, who designed the Paris metro stations, using molds for cast iron, and in so doing, provoked a hostile verdict on his "limp curves".

6 At the Vienna Academy, Jan Kotěra was a student of Otto Wagner, who also taught other leaders of the modern Czech movement (Chochol, Engel, Janák, Plečnik). The master architect expounded his principles of utility and beauty to the exclusion of anything superfluous in *Moderne Architektur*, 1896. In turn, Kotěra taught Gočár, Krejcar, Novotný and Smetana and was the employer of Janák.

7 Other influential foreigners at the time included Charles Rennie Mackintosh, Hendrik Petrus Berlage, Frank Lloyd Wright, Auguster Perret and Henry Van de Velde.

8 Jan Kotěra , O Novém Uměn, Volné Směry (Free Tendencies), IV, 1900, p.192.

9 Rationalism was particularly supported by the Mánes group, and propagated by the periodicals *Styl* and *Volne Směry*. (Cf. also note 17).

10 This coincides with Wagner's idea: "The art of a country reflects not only its material well-being, but above all its intellectual wealth". For Wagner's influence, see note 6.

11 Pavel Janák, From Modern Architecture to Architecture, *Styl*, Prague, vol.2,1910.

12 Bubenec, Král, Vysehrad, Holesovice, Karlin, Královské Vinohrady, Liben, Smíchov, Zizkov.

13 The incorporation of the 37 communes increased the surface of Prague to 66 sq. miles for a population of 670,000 inhabitants.

14 Bohumil Hübschmann, "Le nouveau profil plastique de Prague" (The New Appearance of Prague) in *L'Architecture contemporaine en Tchécoslovaquie*, edited by Krejcar, Orbis, Paris, 1928.

15 Following in the footsteps of Alois Riegl, Max Dvorák, and the work by Camillo Sitte (*Der Städtebau nach seinen Künstlerischen Grundsätzen*, 1889), which was immediately famous and published twice in Germany before 1900, then in French (1902). There was a large movement of opinion in favor of saving Prague's historic areas in the 1890s (in reaction against the "Cleaning Up" policies), and it became institutionalized in 1900 by the founding of the "Society for Old Prague."

16 For a complete account of this period, the reader is invited to consult *L'avant-garde architecturale en Tchécoslovaquie, 1918-1939*, Alena Kubova, Mardaga, Paris, 1992, (237 pp).

17 The periodical *Stavba* (Building, 1922-1938) was published by the "Architects' Club" (influential between the wars) and propagated avant-garde ideas – Rationalism, Purism, Constructivism and Functionalism. The periodical *Stavitel* (The Builder, 1924-1938) was published by the Association of Architects, close to *Stavba* in spirit. The periodical *Styl* (1909-1914 and 1919-1938), published first by Mánes then by the Association of Architects, started out progressive then became conservative in the mid-1920s.

18 Karel Teige, "Images and Prefigurations," in *Musaion* (progressive cultural magazine edited by Čapek), 1921, pp. 52-58. Teige was mainly a theoretician of art and accorded a lot of importance to architecture, mainly in *Stavba*, of which he eventually became chief editor.

19 Karel Teige, "Constructivism and the Liquidation of Art" (Konstruktivismus a likvidace umeni), in *Disk*, n°.2, Spring 1925.

20 Karel Teige, *Život II* (Life II), 1922, a periodical exploring art, and especially architecture.

21 Jaromír Krejcar took the opportunity to justify his earlier 1921 projects for two skyscrapers in working-class Zizkov.

22 Josef Čapek and Karel Čapek (his brother and inventor of the word "robot"), *Malo o Mnohém* (A Little about a Lot), 1923.

23 Some members of Devětsil invented Poeticism in 1923, in opposition to the aesthetics of Romanticism and traditionalism. It champions the abandonment of existing literary forms.

24 Karel Teige, Host 3, 1924. Sober language compared with Nezval's rhetoric: "Socialism, by eliminating individualist anarchy from productive activity, will allow the fullest development of the individual and give him a real right to love and poetry."

25 Adolf Loos was a native of Brno living in Vienna. He published the scathing *Crime and Decoration* in 1908, republished in *L'Esprit nouveau* (The New Spirit) in 1920.

26 Jaroslav Seifert, "All the Beauty of the World" in *Sonnets from Prague*, Index on Censorship 1975, n°3.

27 Kysela was an architect passionate about building, who called one of the great traditions into question, namely houses with massive facades concealing disorder behind. In this connection, in his manifesto *Vers une architecture* (Toward an Architecture), published in 1923, Le Corbusier referred to Prague to strengthen the argument for reinforced concrete in the new architecture: "In Prague an outdated law insists on a thickness of 18 in. for a wall at the top of a house and 6 in. of overhang per story."

28 Kysela, "Crisis of the Capital City and the Different Solutions," *Stavba*, 1929.

29 Pavel Janák, "L'architecture des bâtiments publics" (The Architecture of Public Buildings) in *L'architecture contemporaine*…(see note 14).

30 Ministry of Trade and Industry, 1925-1933. Josef Fanta / Palace of the Ministry of Railways, 1927-1931. Antonín Engel.

31 Palace of the Viennese Banking Union (today Bank of Trade), 1906-1908. Josef Zasche and Alexander Neumann / Municipal library, 1924-1928. Frantizek Roith / Ministry of Agriculture, 1925-1932, Frantizek Roith / Bank of Trade, 1930-1932. Karl Jaray, Ernst von Gotthilf, Alexander Neumann and Rudolf Hildebrand / Czech National Bank, 1928-1939. Frantized Roith.

32 Rebuilding of the Emmaüs Convent, building of the Ministry of Social Affairs and Health, 1923-1939. Bohumil Hübschmann.

33 Quoted by Damjan Prelovsek, "Le métier et la vie d'un homme" in *J Jozě Plečnik architecte 1872-1957*, Pompidou Center Publications, 1986.

34 Rothmayer carried on the master's work after he left Prague, and was particularly concerned with the restoration of the Maria Theresa wing until 1951. He was responsible for a light spiral staircase in granite with steel hoops and copper hood. Rothmayer's work has been studied by in depth by Petr Krajci.

35 Masaryk, 1925, Cf. Note 33.

36 François Burkhardt, "Moderne, postmoderne: Une question d'éthique?", in *Jozě Plečnik*… (see note 33). Some of Burkhardt's analysis of Plecnik's work is repeated here. See also in the same volume: Alena Kubova and Guy Ballangé, "Plecnik et la modernité tchèque."

37 Plecnik was in Prague from 1911 to 1935, but in fact spent much more time in Ljubljana, where he had a teaching post from 1921. He left Prague in 1935 at a time when his Slovenian background made him a target for attacks, and shortly after Masaryk had ceased to be president. Outside Prague most of Plecnik's work is to be found in Vienna (where he had been working for Wagner from 1894) and especially in his native city Ljubljana.

38 An exhibition entitled "Architecture for the New Democracy," 1996, under the patronage of President Kucan of the Slovene Republic and President Havel of the Czech Republic. Curators: Z. Lukes, D. Prelovsek, M. Repa, T. Valena.

39 Raymond Unwin, an English specialist in garden cities, lectured on his ideas in Prague in 1923.

40 F. X. Salda, "La lutte pour le lendeman" (The Struggle for Tomorrow): "charming houses, well kept little houses, in which people can live well and in dignity, or rather in which it is natural to live in this way and incomprehensible to be able to live otherwise". Quoted by Teige in *L'architecture contemporaine*…(see note 14).

41 By way of famous ancestors: the "ancient" – 1859 – "Red House" in London, commissioned by William Morris from his friend Philip Webb, and the project for a house for an art lover by Mackintosh in 1901.

42 Karel Honzík, "Le home moderne" in *L'architecture contemporaine*, (see note 14).

43 Exhibition "die Wohnung", Weissenhof, organized by the Deutscher Werkbund of Stuttgart in 1927.

44 Karel Teige, K Sociologii Architektury, Red, nos 6-7, 1930.

45 Karel Teige, in the preface to *Ladislav Zak, Habitable Landscape*, 1947. An essential book for the redefinition of functionalism, developed during the 1930s.

46 On these post-war matters and the Czechoslovakian territory, see "Ceska architektura, 1945-1995," *Obce architektu*, Prague, 1995 (chapters summarized in English).

47 Ostrava-Poruba, Havirov, Pribram-Brezové Hoty, Stochov, Plzen-Slovany, Ostrov nad Ohrí, Most, Kladno. The master plans of these large estates contain linear buildings perpendicular to each other and usually arranged in a U, taking up and closing off the whole block. Typically they are six-story parallelepipeds with tiled roofs in four sections, rendered brick elevations and neo-Classical design elements (top floor gallery, molded cornices, porched entrance with pediments and columns, etc.).

48 Jirí Novotny, Urban Policy of Prague in Prague… (Note 49).

49 For a detailed description of heritage issues in Prague in the 19th and 20th centuries, see the multi-authored work *Prague – Avenir d'une ville historique capitale* (Prague, History of a Historic Capital City), l'Aube publications, Paris, 1992.

50 Zdenek Lukes, "Modern Architecture in Bohemia," in *Historic Monuments*, no 188, 1993.

51 Zdenek Lukes, idem

52 Among others: Prague Castle and surroundings, Troja Castle, Hvezda Pavilion, Strahov and Saint Agnes convents and the Schwarzenberg, Wallenstein, Hrzan, Kaiserstein and Lichtenstejn Palaces.

53 Ivo Hlobil, "One Hundred Years of Preserving the Historical Towns of Bohemia" in *Prague*… (see note 49).

54 Jacques Derrida, "Générations d'une ville: mémoire, prophétie, responsabilités" in *Prague*… (see note 49).

Photographic Credits

Printed by Eurografica
September 2002
Vicenza - ITALY